WOMEN OF COURAGE

*Profiles of five
remarkable Americans:*

SUSAN B. ANTHONY
JANE ADDAMS
MARY MC LEOD BETHUNE
AMELIA EARHART
MARGARET MEAD

BY DOROTHY NATHAN

WOMEN OF COURAGE

ILLUSTRATED BY CAROLYN CATHER

RANDOM HOUSE   NEW YORK

4 366

Grateful acknowledgment is made to:

*The Macmillan Company for permission to use on pages 41 and 51
quotations from* Twenty Years at Hull-House *by Jane Addams.*

*The Vanguard Press for permission to use on pages 86, 87, 94, 99, 100,
112, 113 quotations from* Mary McLeod Bethune *by Catherine Owens
Peare. Copyright, 1951, by Catherine Owens Peare. Quoted by permission of the publishers, The Vanguard Press.*

*Harcourt, Brace & World, Inc. for permission to use on pages 119–20,
126–27, 128, 129, 132 quotations from* Soaring Wings; A Biography of
Amelia Earhart *by George Palmer Putnam, copyright, 1939, by George
Palmer Putnam. Reprinted by permission of Harcourt, Brace & World,
Inc.*

*Harcourt, Brace & World, Inc. for permission to use on pages 130,
137–39, 142 quotations from* Last Flight *by Amelia Earhart, copyright,
1937, by Harcourt, Brace & World, Inc.*

*The Bobbs-Merrill Company, Inc. for permission to use on page 151 two
lines of "The Raggedy Man" from* Joyful Poems for Children *by James
Whitcomb Riley, copyright 1946, 1960 by The Bobbs-Merrill Company,
Inc., reprinted by special permission of the publishers.*

*The World Publishing Company for permission to use on pages 158 and
174–75 quotations from* People and Places *by Margaret Mead.*

CONTENTS

INTRODUCTION

This is a book about the lives of five women.

They were alike in being women of unusual courage, but the lives they led were very different. Susan B. Anthony fought down the line for woman's right to have rights. Jane Addams walked out of her comfortable private parlor to make Chicago's slums her home. Mary McLeod Bethune, like a conscience, drilled away at prejudices which kept Negro children from growing up to share the good things in American life. Amelia Earhart flew airplanes, proving that women as well as men have spirit to dare and do. Margaret Mead traveled to the corners of the world in her search for the secrets of human nature.

There are numberless extraordinary American women whose lives are woven into the bright pattern of our country. These five stand out for their boldness and imagination.

WOMEN OF COURAGE

SUSAN B. ANTHONY

"Failure Is Impossible"

1

When Susan B. Anthony began her career of reform, crowds hissed her for saying women are entitled to the same political rights as men. Drunks threatened her with guns. She was strung up and burned in effigy. Clergymen denounced her as a dangerous crank. Newspapers made fun of her in cartoons that showed a half-dressed, masculine-looking hag smoking a thick black cigar.

But for more than sixty years, against all odds, Miss Anthony fought tooth and nail for her ideas. By the time she died—on March 13, 1906, at the age of 86—she had earned a place as one of America's leaders.

Susan Brownell Anthony was born on February 15, 1820, in an era when girls were raised like hothouse flowers. They were supposed to be shy and retiring. Outdoor exercise such as running, jumping, or bicycle riding was unheard of. Indeed it was impossible: A girl was a prisoner in her clothes. A young lady of thirteen wore a stiff corset which squeezed her body into whatever shape was the fashion that year. Then there was a corset cover and long drawers. Next came five or six heavy, quilted, stiffly starched petticoats. Finally there was a dress with high neck, long sleeves, tight bodice, and full skirt which swept the ground.

In this age a woman's aim in life was to marry, and her occupation was housekeeping and child-rearing. No high degree of education was needed, and none was offered. Girls learned to cook and sew, make butter and cheese, spin and weave.

Women who did not marry were pitied or joked about. Few people really believed anyone who said she preferred to remain single. For how could anybody "prefer" not to have a husband to support her and give her a position in the community? Women were not citizens, but subjects. They did not appear in public places without an escort. And because they had no rights before the law, they could not buy a business, or sign a contract, or inherit money, or own land, or even be legal guardians of their own children.

If a woman had to work, her wages were paid directly to her husband. In general people accepted the idea that women were born inferior. Like slaves, idiots, and criminals, they were not allowed to vote.

Women did not take jobs, but they worked hard at home. Daniel Anthony, Susan's father, was a well-to-do Quaker businessman. He owned a general store and a cotton mill in the pleasant countryside near Adams, Massachusetts. Mr. Anthony was a generous man and he loved his wife, Lucy. Yet she was expected to run her household, which then included three little daughters and eleven boarding mill workers, with only the part-time help of a thirteen-year-old schoolgirl.

So Lucy Anthony cooked, cleaned, washed, and ironed. She baked bread and cake in a brick oven and prepared meals for sixteen people on a hearth in front of the fireplace. Spinning, weaving, knitting, and mending took their part of each long working day. And there is no record that Lucy Anthony ever complained. In the early nineteenth century hers was "the natural lot of the female."

Her husband, Daniel, lived by his conscience first, the rules of society second. He had shocked his Quaker neighbors by marrying Lucy Read. Lucy was his childhood sweetheart, but she was not a Quaker. The neighbors were shocked again when independent-minded Daniel Anthony broke the "dress plain" rule in winter time. He was cold and woolen scarves were warm, so he wore woolen scarves—bright ones which kept the biting wind from his ears, but not the Quakers' scoldings.

Mr. Anthony was so free in his ideas that he even

shocked his wife. He brought his children up to believe that girls were different from boys, but not inferior. Once he permitted twelve-year-old Susan to work in his mill, taking the place of a "spooler" woman who was ill. Susan was delighted. For two weeks she faithfully wound cotton thread onto spools. Mr. Anthony paid her the same salary the "spooler" would have earned: $1.50 a week. Susan gave half of what she earned to her sister Hannah, and spent her own share on some pale blue cups and saucers for her mother.

One evening at dinner Susan said to her father, "Why isn't Sally Ann in charge of the spoolers at the mill? She can untangle the thread better than Elijah."

Mr. Anthony shook his head. Such a notion was unthinkable even to a man with advanced ideas. "It would never do," he said. "A woman could never be the boss."

Susan's schooling had started in Battenville, New York, where the family moved when she was six. At first she attended the district school, an old-fashioned one-room building where all the children sat on long wooden benches fastened around the walls.

Susan quickly learned to read and do simple sums. But one day she surprised the teacher by asking if she could learn long division. He refused. For one thing, he wasn't too sure of the subject himself. For another, why would a female want to stuff her head with useless information?

But Mr. Anthony took a different view. He decided

his children needed a better education than the district school offered. So he set aside a room on the second floor of his fine, fifteen-room brick house, and furnished it with such up-to-date equipment as separate stools for each pupil. He invited his neighbors' children to attend. As the first teacher, he hired a young woman who had studied in an advanced "female seminary."

Miss Mary Perkins introduced many teaching ideas which were new in that day. Of course, like all well-brought-up youngsters, Susan and the other girls were taught to make bed quilts and to hem ruffles. But they also learned to recite poetry and do long division. Miss Perkins even gave them books which had been written especially for school children.

Mr. Anthony believed that his daughters, like his sons, must be trained to be self-supporting. He wanted Susan and her sister Guelma to be well qualified to teach, since teaching was almost the only genteel occupation open to women. So when his two oldest daughters were in their late teens he enrolled them in Miss Deborah Moulson's Seminary for Females, to complete their education. Susan was sent to the boarding school in the fall of 1837 to join Guelma, who had gone there the previous year.

Miss Moulson's Seminary was near Philadelphia, Pennsylvania. Seventeen-year-old Susan had never been so far from home in her life, and she was extremely lonely. In 1837 postage for a letter cost eighteen cents. Susan would surely have run up quite a sum had it not been for the fortunate fact that Mr. Anthony was now the postmaster at Battenville. This entitled him and his family to free use of the mails. Guelma scolded, "Susan, thee writes too much; thee should learn to be concise." But Susan kept on writing.

Miss Moulson had strict rules for the writing of letters. First, Susan had to write each letter on a slate. Then the teacher corrected it. Then Susan copied it on foolscap paper, using a quill pen. If she made an ink blot, she had to recopy it. She had to write tiny letters because a bold handwriting was not ladylike.

No wonder it took several days to get out a letter. No wonder Susan's letters sounded stiff:

Beloved Parents:

. . . The difference in weather is quite material between this and our northern clime. Snow commenced falling about 12 o'clock today and continued till evening . . . The cause of my neglecting to write last week was not an absence of this mind from home, but that it is obliged to occupy every moment in studies.

Although proper letters written by young females were supposed to deal with safe subjects, such as weather and health, Susan managed to tell a bit about life at school. Once a visiting teacher came to talk about science, and Susan wrote, "He had a microscope through which we had the pleasure of viewing the dust from the wings of a butterfly . . ."

Another time, a letter from home told Susan about a young friend who had just married a widower with six children. Susan made an entry in her diary: "I should think any female would rather live and die an old maid."

Susan tried hard to do her best at school, but somehow her best was never good enough for strict old Miss Moulson. Once she scolded Susan so severely that the girl burst into tears and rushed to her room. She wrote in her diary that night, "If I am such a vile sinner, I would that I might feel it myself. Indeed, I do consider myself such a bad creature that I can not see any who seems worse."

What was her vile sin? She had been unable to repeat to Miss Moulson the rule for dotting an i!

One day Susan spied spider webs on the classroom ceiling. Like any good housekeeper, she fetched a broom to sweep them down. But even on tiptoe the high ceiling was out of reach. So Susan pulled the teacher's desk under the cobwebs and stood on that. Alas! A hinge broke. Miss Moulson came storming in. She gave Susan such a dressing-down that years later Miss Anthony wrote, "Not once, in the sixty years that have passed, has the thought of that day come to my mind without making me turn cold and sick at heart."

In the spring of 1838 Mr. Anthony came to Philadelphia to fetch his daughters home. He told them sad news: His business had fallen on hard times. He was bankrupt, and would have to sell off everything he owned to pay his creditors.

Mr. Anthony's factory, store, and beautiful home were sold at auction. Mrs. Anthony saw all her furnishings go, even the set of silver teaspoons her parents had given her as a wedding present. The children's schoolbooks were sold, the boys' pocket-knives, Mr. and Mrs. Anthony's steel-rimmed spectacles, everybody's clothing, even the kitchen supplies of flour, tea, coffee, and sugar.

Susan wrote in her diary: "I probably shall never go to school again, and all the advancement which I hereafter make must be by my own exertions."

In March of 1839 the family moved to a small village called Hardscrabble, and Susan's journal became a record of keeping house. "Did a large washing . . . Spent today at the spinning wheel . . . Baked 21 loaves of bread . . . Wove three yards of carpet yesterday . . ."

But young people cannot stay sad. Soon the young Anthonys were enjoying quilting bees and apple-paring parties and sleigh rides. Sometimes fifteen or twenty couples would ride in long horse-and-buggy processions to a nearby village to dine or picnic on a pleasant riverbank. Guelma got married. So did Hannah. Susan had many admirers and several offers of marriage, but she turned away from them. She seemed to feel she had some other serious purpose in life.

Susan often argued with Guelma's new husband, Aaron McLean, defending her belief that girls and

boys should be educated the same way. One day, when Susan had baked some delicious cream biscuits for supper, Aaron said, "I'd rather see a woman make such biscuits as these than solve the knottiest problem in algebra."

"There is no reason why she should not be able to do both," said Susan.

2

In the fall of 1839 Susan took the first of a series of teaching jobs away from home. She taught almost without interruption until 1845, living frugally and sending money home to help her father.

Gradually Mr. Anthony's prospects improved. In 1845 he moved his family to Rochester, New York, where he again became prosperous.

As soon as Susan did not have to send money home, she began to spend her salary on clothes. "I have a new pearl straw gypsy hat," she wrote, "trimmed in white ribbon with fringe on one edge and a pink satin stripe on the other, with a few white roses and green leaves for inside trimming."

She dressed her thick chestnut hair in a new style, four braids wound around a big shell comb. She bought a plum-colored dress "which everybody admits to be the sweetest thing entirely," and she wondered in her diary if her sisters "do not feel rather sad because they are married and can not have nice clothes."

Whenever she could, Susan went home to visit. Her father's house was generally full of lively people discussing the issues of the day. Often there would be fifteen or twenty guests at Sunday dinner, with Susan hurrying back and forth between the kitchen and the dining room. She wanted to help her mother but hated to miss a word of the conversation.

As Susan listened, she longed to fight the wrongs of society. She began to take an active part in battles against slavery and drunkenness. She attended meetings of the Abolitionists, who wanted to abolish slavery. She also joined an organization called Daughters of Temperance, which urged passage of laws to regulate the liquor industry.

Susan met other women with the same interests— Mrs. Elizabeth Cady Stanton, Mrs. Lucy Stone (Blackwell), Mrs. Lucretia Mott, Reverend Antoinette Brown, Mrs. Amelia Bloomer, and many others. With her father's warm encouragement, Susan found herself giving "every power of her being" to reform.

The first Woman's Rights Convention which Susan ever attended began on September 8, 1852, in Syracuse, New York. The audience (largely women, of course) clapped heartily as speakers asked, "Why are women forbidden to own property? Why are they refused the advantages of higher education? Why are they not man's equal before the law?" The Convention demanded free speech and the right of women to vote.

The reporter for the Syracuse *Journal* must have

felt friendly, for he wrote that no person could deny there was great talent attending the convention.

"The appearance of all the ladies was modest and unassuming. . . . Business was brought forward . . . and discussed . . . in a spirit becoming true women . . ."

But the Syracuse *Star* named it the "Tomfoolery Convention."

For months after the convention ended, there was "a raging tempest of battle" in pulpits across the land. Ministers pointed out the terrible spectacle of immodest females who abandoned their families to speak in public. Any men who encouraged such women were not true friends, said the ministers; they were simply dragging womanhood from the high pedestal on which it belonged, and trampling it in the dust.

Most ladies loved this kind of talk. They sat in church pews adjusting their lace shawls, while the ribbons of their bonnets nodded up and down as though to say, "Beautiful thoughts, perfectly beautiful."

But the handful of reform-minded women did not want to sit up on a pedestal. They wanted to get down and stir around and live comfortable lives. They believed tightly laced corsets and weighty dresses were just another tyranny women lived under to please men. By wearing sensible clothes they would dramatize their rights. After all, physical comfort should be the privilege of every human being.

Mrs. Elizabeth Cady Stanton and Lucy Stone convinced Susan that dress reform was an important part of the woman's rights movement. Susan reluctantly put away her pretty clothes and stitched herself one of the new costumes. It consisted of a loose dress with a pair of matching Turkish-style trousers underneath, neatly gathered at the ankles for modesty. Amelia Bloomer, who published a magazine, urged all women to try this comfortable new "American costume."

Only a handful did. Most men and women denounced "that shocking Bloomer outfit" in a storm that blew coldly from one end of the country to the other.

Whenever Miss Anthony or any of her friends appeared in public, crowds of men and boys would quickly gather to jeer and throw stones. Often they tagged at the heels of the embarrassed lady as she walked down the street. Sometimes the unhappy Bloomerite would have to hide until her tormentors drifted away and she could sneak home through back alleys. Other women in the community, of course, cut her cold. Often her own family refused to be seen with her in public.

Susan endured the humiliation bravely, although it cost her many private tears. But she felt she must be true to her principles, so she wore the hated garment for a year and a half.

In the summer of 1853 Susan attended a meeting of the New York State Teachers' Association. She sat impatiently for two days while the men in the audience spoke on and on about why the teaching profession

was not as highly respected as that of doctor, lawyer, or minister. Two-thirds of the teachers at this meeting were women, but because of their sex they could not speak in public or vote on any question before the meeting. They could only pay their dues and listen obediently.

Finally Miss Anthony could not sit still another moment. She popped up and said, "Mr. Chairman!"

A shocked hush fell. Every neck swiveled around to see the hussy who dared break an iron rule of social behavior by calling public attention to herself. They saw a slender, serious young woman of thirty-three, dressed in the odious Bloomer costume.

"What will the lady have?" asked the chairman.

Susan's heart thumped a tattoo. Her knees shook. "It seems to me you fail to comprehend the cause of the disrespect of which you complain," she managed to say in her pleasantly low, clear voice. "Do you not see that so long as society says woman has not brains enough to be a doctor, lawyer, or minister, but has plenty to be a teacher, every man of you who condescends to teach . . . admits . . . that he has no more brains than a woman?"

Miss Anthony sat down. The lady in the next seat whispered loudly to a companion, "Disgraceful creature!" Then she carefully drew her watered-silk hoop skirt aside from possible contamination by Miss Anthony's Bloomer dress.

More sharply than ever, Miss Anthony saw that the battle for woman's rights was going to be long and hard. And the main issue was the vote. When women could vote, the other reforms they wanted would follow.

Not long afterward, Susan decided that the Bloomer outfit was a mistake. It called attention to a speaker's clothes instead of permitting the audience to concentrate on her words. It was smarter to fight for one reform at a time.

Susan gave up teaching, she abandoned the Bloomer outfit, and for the rest of her very long life she became a gadfly who dedicated "every day of her time, every dollar of her money, every power of her being," to the cause of equal rights for women.

Miss Anthony began the fight in her own state of

New York. She traveled about talking on woman's rights, selling tracts, and gathering signatures on a petition. She planned to present the signatures at a meeting of the State Legislature, New York's law-making body, urging its members to change the law so women could own property.

Miss Anthony's tour began in the town of Mayville on the damp evening of December 26, 1854. Her first small audience gathered in a courthouse lit by four pounds of candles she had bought for fifty-six cents. Later, in other communities, Miss Anthony spoke in town halls or in churches. But not infrequently officials would refuse her the use of a regular meeting place. Then she would hunt up a fair-minded man— a hotel owner, perhaps, who would let her lecture in his dining room.

This was no pleasure trip. The winter was unusually snowy. Many towns were at the far end of a long, cold sleigh ride. Inns in those days did not have hot water at the turn of a faucet, or steam heat to warm a bedroom. Often Miss Anthony had to break the ice in her water pitcher before she could wash.

Many people in her audiences had never before heard a woman speaking in public. Some men scolded Miss Anthony for making a spectacle of herself. Others abused her for trying, as they thought, to break up their happy homes. But many listened seriously to her earnest arguments, and even said that they and their wives and daughters would help. By the time Miss Anthony returned home to rest after her five-month tour, she had visited fifty-four counties and sold 20,000 tracts.

But more signatures were needed on the petitions to the Legislature. In January 1856 Miss Anthony and a companion bravely set forth once again. This winter was even more cold and more snowy than the last. And again Miss Anthony saw rich examples of the kind of injustice she was fighting to correct. She wrote to her mother:

> Wendte's Station, Jan. 14, 1856
> 12½ o'clock pm

> . . . We stopped at a little tavern where the landlady was not yet twenty and had a baby fifteen months old. Her supper dishes were not washed and her baby was crying, but she was equal to the occasion. She rocked the little thing to sleep, washed the dishes and got our supper . . .

> She gave us her warm bedroom to sleep in, and on a row of pegs hung the loveliest embroidered petticoats and baby clothes, all the work of that young woman's fingers, while on a rack was her ironing perfectly done, wrought undersleeves, baby dresses, embroidered underwear, etc.

> She prepared a six o'clock breakfast for us, fried pork, mashed potatoes, mince pie, and for me, at my especial request, a plate of delicious baked sweet apples and a pitcher of rich milk.

> Now for the moral of this story: When we came to pay our bill, the dolt of a husband took the money and put it in his pocket. He had not lifted a hand to lighten that woman's burdens, but had sat and talked with the men in the bar room, not even caring for the baby, yet the law gives him the

right to every dollar she earns, and when she needs two cents to buy a darning needle she has to ask him and explain what she wants it for.

In February Miss Anthony traveled to the state capital at Albany to present to the Legislature the fruit of her two years of hard work. Her petitions had been signed by some 10,000 women, who asked to be given the legal right to control their own income and have custody of their own children.

The legislators were not impressed. One speaker said, "Are we going to give the least countenance to claims so preposterous, disgraceful, and criminal? Are we going to put the stamp of truth upon the libel here set forth that men and women . . . are to be equal? We *know* that God created man as the representative of the race."

A committee of the Legislature studied Miss Anthony's request and then made its report. Senators slapped their knees and roared with laughter as the chairman announced: ". . . the ladies always have the best place and choicest tidbit at the table. They have the best seats in the cars . . . the warmest place in winter and the coolest in summer. . . . A lady's dress costs three times as much as that of a gentleman and . . . with the prevailing fashion, one lady occupies three times as much space in the world as a gentleman. It has thus appeared . . . that if there is any inequality or oppression in the case, the gentlemen are the sufferers."

Friends urged Miss Anthony to stop crusading. "Let the world alone a while," wrote Mrs. Elizabeth Cady Stanton. "You need rest too. We cannot bring about a moral revolution in a day or a year."

But Miss Anthony knew she must continue her work, in season and out, publicly and privately. She wrote back to Mrs. Stanton, "All this is but the noise and dust of the wagon bringing the harvest home. These things must be, and happy are they who see clearly to the end."

In her diary went a note: "Cautious, careful people, always casting about to preserve their reputation and social standing, never can bring about a reform."

And she continued to battle. She traveled to Troy to address a meeting of the New York State Teachers' Association on the subject, "Why the Sexes Should be Educated Together." This was a shocking idea to many people. After Miss Anthony's speech the president of the Teachers' Association said to her, "Madam, that was a splendid production . . . I could not have asked for a single thing different . . . but I would rather have followed my wife or daughter to Greenwood cemetery than to have had her stand there before this [mixed] audience and deliver that address."

Undaunted, Miss Anthony planned a new lecture, "The True Woman," to express her firm belief that a woman must not "sacrifice all for the love of one man," and adjust the rest of her life to his whims.

Every woman, said Miss Anthony, has a personality and talents of her own. She is entitled to advance in learning, in the arts, in science, and in business. Miss Anthony went so far as to believe that a woman who entered into an unfortunate marriage should be entitled to secure a divorce if she wished it.

By the 1860s there were hundreds of Americans who believed in the right of women to vote. They hoped that when the Civil War was over, women would be enfranchised along with former slaves. (Miss Anthony had thrown herself into the cause of freedom for Negroes with all her customary zeal.) But the Fourteenth Amendment, which became law on July 28, 1868, granted citizenship to freedmen without mentioning women. In vain did Miss Anthony and others point out that women were citizens too. "Aren't women people?" they asked.

And in spite of the Fourteenth Amendment, Southern states still kept their voting booths closed to Negroes. Clearly, another amendment was needed —one which would spell out in unmistakable terms that every Negro citizen also had the right to vote.

The woman's rights leaders threw their weight toward a Fifteenth Amendment. Again they hoped that this time Negroes and women would be enfranchised together. Miss Anthony became the president of a new organization, the Woman's Suffrage Association of America, dedicated to forcing the United States to recognize the political rights of woman.

On March 30, 1870, a Fifteenth Amendment became the law of the land. It said: "The right of citizens of the United States to vote shall not be denied or abridged by the United States or by any State on account of race, color, or previous condition of servitude."

Again, there was no mention of the sex of the citizen whose right to vote must not be denied. Miss Anthony decided the time was ripe for a bold new attack.

On November 1, 1872, Susan and her sisters Guelma, Hannah, and Mary calmly walked into a

shoemaker's shop that was the polling place in their election district of Rochester. "We are here to register for the vote," said Miss Anthony to the flabbergasted election inspector.

"Impossible!" he said. "It is not legal for women to vote. We can not accept your registration."

From her handbag Miss Anthony whipped out a copy of the Constitution of the United States. All three election inspectors gathered around as she slowly read aloud the Fourteenth and Fifteenth amendments. Then she challenged the inspectors to show her where it said women were specifically left

out. The men sputtered and argued in vain. At last they reluctantly registered the four women.

Miss Anthony was delighted. So far, so good, but she didn't stop there. She bustled about the city and rounded up twelve more women who were willing to register, and then another thirty-four. She also talked to about twenty lawyers. At last she found one who agreed to aid her if she got into trouble by voting.

When election day came, not all of the women who had registered were brave enough to vote. But Susan Brownell Anthony voted. So did her three sisters and eleven other sturdy friends.

Their action made headlines all over the country. Some newspapers were friendly. Many were not. Angry editorials poured off the presses to denounce the fifteen women but especially their leader. One newspaper declared that Miss Anthony's lawlessness *proved* women were not fit to vote! Statements appeared, calling for her arrest. Miss Anthony must be brought to trial for her crime of voting. If this action of hers went unpunished, every woman in America from that day forward could simply register and vote!

Now the battle lines were drawn. The government could ignore its gadfly no longer. As she would not be brushed off, she would have to be slapped down.

On Monday, November 18, United States Deputy Marshal E. J. Keeney rang the Anthony doorbell and said, "Miss Anthony, I have a warrant for your arrest."

Miss Anthony held out her wrists and said, "Handcuff me!"

The unhappy marshal, putting his top hat back on his head, pretended not to hear. Together they walked to the corner and got on the horse-drawn streetcar that would take them to the office of the United States Commissioner. When the conductor came around for their fares, Miss Anthony said loudly, "This gentleman is escorting me to jail. Ask *him* for my fare." People in the car stared. Marshal Keeney's face became the color of boiled shrimp.

There were several legal delays before Miss Anthony found herself in the Commissioner's office with the other fourteen ladies who had voted, as well as the election inspectors who had permitted them to vote. Miss Anthony's lawyer, Henry B. Selden, was there too.

After arguments on both sides were heard, the election commissioner ruled that the women must come to trial in a federal court. He ordered each defendant to be held in bail of $500.

Reporters who were present hurried off to file their stories. One wrote, "The majority of these law-breakers were elderly, matronly-looking women with thoughtful faces, just the sort one would like to see in charge of one's sickroom, considerate, patient, kindly."

Fourteen of the women paid their bail, but not Susan. Instead she filed a legal paper, called a writ of habeas corpus, which demanded her release. A hearing on the demand was held in an Albany federal court. The court not only rejected the writ of habeas corpus, it ordered bail increased from $500 to $1,000. Miss Anthony stubbornly declared she would sit in jail until the day of the trial rather than pay this sum. To her disappointment, Mr. Selden insisted on paying it for her. "I could not see a lady I respected put in jail," he said.

Trial was set for the month of May in the city of Rochester, county of Monroe, state of New York. This gave Miss Anthony one month. She decided to use it talking to the people of Monroe County. She wanted them to understand the points on which she based her right to vote.

Miss Anthony visited twenty-nine post-office districts in Monroe County and spoke twenty-nine times on "The Equal Right of All Citizens to the Ballot." When she finished talking she would ask her audience to tell her if they thought she had broken the law.

United States District Attorney Richard Crowley heard about the lecture tour and angrily declared that it would now be impossible to select an honest jury in Monroe County. Miss Anthony replied, "Does it prejudice a jury to read and explain the Constitution of the United States?"

But when trial time drew near, the district attorney obtained an order transferring the case to another county because Miss Anthony had "corrupted" the people of Monroe County. The trial was reset for June 17 in Canandaigua, county of Ontario.

This gave Miss Anthony another twenty-two days. She and a friend, Mrs. Matilda Joslyn Gage, descended upon Ontario County. Miss Anthony spoke twenty-one times on the subject, "Is It a Crime for a Citizen of the United States to Vote?" Mrs. Gage spoke sixteen times on "The United States on Trial, Not Susan B. Anthony."

June 17, 1873, was a sunny day in the little up-state town of Canandaigua. Its second-floor court-room was filled to the rafters with judge, jury, lawyer, defendant, reporters, friends of the defendant, and friends and enemies of the woman's rights movement from all over the country.

Wearing a simple silk dress and a blue bonnet with a dotted veil, Susan sat quietly while her lawyer addressed the judge and jury in a carefully reasoned three-hour argument.

"Women have the same interest that men have in the establishment and maintenance of good government," said Mr. Selden. "They are to the same extent as men bound to obey the laws; they suffer to the same extent by bad laws, and profit to the same extent by good laws; and upon principles of equal justice, as it would seem, should be allowed, equally with men, to express their preference in the choice of lawmakers and rulers."

Next came a two-hour speech by the district attorney. He argued that even if Miss Anthony had voted in good faith, believing the Constitution gave her the right to vote, what she believed was not the issue. The fact was that her voting violated a law of the United States. She was therefore guilty of a crime.

Then Judge Ward Hunt took a manuscript out of his desk drawer and began to read it to the jury. Miss Anthony was astonished. How could the judge write his message to the jury before he had even heard the arguments in the case?

"If the Fifteenth Amendment had contained the word 'sex' the argument of the defendant would have been potent . . ." read the thin-lipped little judge in his dry voice. "The Fourteenth Amendment gives no right to a woman to vote, and the voting of Miss Anthony was in violation of the law . . .

"There was no ignorance of any fact," he continued, "but all the facts being known, she undertook to settle a principle in her own person . . ."

And so, he concluded, ". . . the jury should be directed to find a verdict of guilty."

Lawyer Selden leaped to his feet. "The jury must be permitted to bring in its own verdict," he said.

Judge Hunt spoke again, still addressing the jury: "The question . . . is wholly a question . . . of law, and I have decided as a question of law . . . that under the Fourteenth Amendment which Miss Anthony claims protects her, she was not protected in a right to vote . . . and therefore I direct that you find a verdict of guilty."

Again Henry Selden stood to demand that the

jury be permitted to bring in its own verdict.

No reply from the judge. "Take the verdict," he snapped to the clerk of the court.

"Gentlemen of the jury," said the clerk, "hearken to your verdict as the Court has recorded it. You say you find the defendant guilty of the offense whereof she stands indicted, and so say you all."

"I demand that each juryman be polled separately," said Mr. Selden.

Judge Hunt turned to the jurymen. Not one of them had spoken a word. "Gentlemen of the jury, you are discharged," he said.

The next day Mr. Selden asked for a new trial on the grounds that Miss Anthony had been denied her right of trial by jury. Judge Hunt refused the motion. He ordered Miss Anthony to stand. "Has the prisoner anything to say why sentence shall not be pronounced?" he asked.

"Yes, your honor," said Miss Anthony, "I have many things to say; for in your ordered verdict of guilty you have trampled under foot every vital principle of our government. My natural rights, my civil rights, my political rights, my judicial rights, are all alike ignored . . ."

"The court can not listen to a rehearsal of argument which the prisoner's counsel has already consumed three hours in presenting," said Judge Hunt.

But Susan went right on: "May it please your honor, I am not arguing the question, but simply stating the reasons why sentence cannot, in justice, be pronounced against me.

"Your denial of my citizen's right to vote is the denial of my right of consent as one of the governed, the denial of my right of representation as one of the taxed, the denial of my right to a trial by a jury of my peers as an offender against the law; therefore, the denial of my sacred right to life, liberty, property and——"

"The Court can not allow the prisoner to go on," Judge Hunt interrupted testily.

Susan continued: "But your honor would not deny me this one and only poor privilege of protest against this high-handed outrage upon my citizen's right . . ."

"The Court must insist—the prisoner has been tried according to the established forms of law."

"Yes, your honor," said Miss Anthony, "but by forms of law all made by men, interpreted by men, administered by men, in favor of men and against women . . ."

Judge Hunt, his voice tight with controlled anger, cut her off: "The Court orders the prisoner to sit down. It will not allow another word."

Miss Anthony went right on talking: "When I was brought before your honor for trial, I hoped for a broad and liberal interpretation of the Constitution . . . But failing to get this justice . . . I ask not leniency at your hands but rather the full rigor of the law."

"The Court must insist——" shouted the judge.

Miss Anthony sat down.

"The prisoner will stand up," said Judge Hunt. Miss Anthony stood up.

"The sentence of the Court is that you pay a fine of $100 and the costs of the prosecution."

". . . I will never pay a dollar of your unjust penalty . . ." protested Miss Anthony. "And I shall earnestly and persistently continue to urge all women to the practical recognition of the old Revolutionary maxim, 'Resistance to tyranny is obedience to God.'"

"Madam," replied Judge Hunt, "the Court will not order you to stand committed until the fine is paid."

He stood, and the trial was over.

3

Feeling about the trial ran high. Even people who disapproved of Miss Anthony were outraged at the way Judge Hunt had hurried the jury into a decision. They agreed that it endangered the freedom of every person in the country when any judge tampered with any accused person's right to a fair trial by jury.

Lawyers noted how clever Judge Hunt was in not ordering Miss Anthony to "stand committed"—that is, either to pay the fine or go to jail. For if she were imprisoned, she could appeal her case to the Supreme Court of the United States. As Judge Hunt had arranged it, a legal appeal was impossible. The most Miss Anthony could do was refuse to pay the fine and then see what happened.

Miss Anthony did refuse to pay the fine, and nothing happened. Nor did the government ever bring any of her fourteen friends to trial. But offers of financial help and letters of sympathy poured in upon Miss Anthony from acquaintances and strangers all over the country. So she tucked up her sleeves and got on with her work. She was sure now: The only way to enfranchise woman was by constitutional amendment.

Year after year, woman suffrage bills were introduced before the legislatures of various states. Some passed. Some did not. Miss Anthony gave these bills, and the friends who were supporting them, her whole-hearted encouragement. But she herself worked hardest for a federal law which would be binding on all the states. As president of the National American Woman Suffrage Association, she presided over annual conventions. Year after year she urged an amendment to the Constitution which would spell out woman's right to vote.

It would be impossible to mark the moment when the tide turned, but as the years rolled on, great waves of admiration and respect swept in upon Miss Anthony. Bouquets and testimonials replaced the hurled tomatoes of yesteryear. Politicians asked her advice. Newspapers invited her to write editorials. Every time she spoke at the Chicago World's Fair during the summer of 1893, men and women alike climbed on their chairs, threw hats, gloves, and handkerchiefs into the air, and cheered roundly before she said a word. The trim, gray-haired lady with a red shawl around her shoulders had become a symbol of the woman suffrage movement.

"Spring is not heralded in Washington by the arrival of the robin," said one Washington newspaper, "but by the appearance of Miss Anthony's red shawl."

In 1900, when Miss Anthony was 80, she turned the presidency of her beloved woman suffrage organization over to a younger woman, Mrs. Carrie Chapman Catt. "Failure is impossible," she told the army of women who would carry on.

And she was right. On August 26, 1920, exactly one century from the year of Susan's birth, a Nineteenth Amendment was added to the law of the land. This amendment, often called "the Susan B. Anthony Amendment," says:

> *The right of citizens of the United States to vote shall not be denied or abridged by the United States or by any State on account of sex.*

Although Miss Anthony did not live to see the final victory, there were many changes to gladden her old warrior's heart. By the turn of the century, for instance, women and girls were freely riding bicycles—some of them wearing short skirts or even bloomers. "I rejoice every time I see a woman ride by on a wheel," said Miss Anthony. "It gives her a feeling of self-reliance and independence the moment she takes her seat; and away she goes, the picture of untrammeled womanhood."

Girls were going to school together with boys now, and several men's colleges accepted women students. But Miss Anthony wanted young women to be able to attend *any* college that young men could attend.

She trained her guns on the University of Rochester in her own home town. She badgered the trustees for several years. At last they agreed to admit a small number of women—provided a fund of $50,000 could be raised within one year.

With her usual energy, Susan got together a fund-raising committee. She and the other committee members began calling on wealthy businessmen, University graduates, and trustees. The money came in very slowly. Most of these men were not friendly to the idea of women students.

Other matters claimed her attention, and a year slipped by. A younger brother, Merritt Anthony, died suddenly, and Susan went out to Kansas to attend his funeral. She had just returned to Rochester when she received a distress call from the secretary of the fund committee. Their time would run out the next afternoon! They were still $8,000 short!

Susan spent a sleepless night, mapping a campaign. And the campaign began with her sister Mary before breakfast next morning.

Mary had provided in her will for a $2,000 gift to

the University of Rochester. "Give the money now," urged Miss Anthony. "Don't wait, or the girls may never be admitted."

Mary agreed. Then Miss Anthony got into her carriage and began visiting friends and acquaintances. A pastor pledged $2,000. An old friend gave $2,000. The hot September day wore on. Miss Anthony called on stores, offices, banks, factories. In vain. Not another dollar could she get.

In desperation, she drove to the home of Mr. Samuel Wilder. He was an old friend who had contributed a sum earlier in the year. Quickly Susan explained her emergency: The Board of Trustees was already in session to cancel their offer. She needed a final amount of $2,000.

With Mr. Wilder's guarantee in her hand, Miss Anthony raced off through lengthening afternoon shadows. Trustees' eyebrows rose with astonishment as she swept into their meeting room. Clearly, nobody was expecting her.

Shaking with excitement, Miss Anthony presented her pledges for $8,000. With careful deliberation the trustees examined each name and amount. Then they whispered with one another. At last the chairman said to Miss Anthony, "We are sorry, but Mr. Wilder's guarantee is not acceptable. We know he is in poor health. If he were to die shortly, his estate could not be held for $2,000."

For a moment Miss Anthony was stumped. But only for a moment. Then she said, "Well, gentlemen,

I may as well confess. I am the guarantor, but I asked Mr. Wilder to lend me his name so that this question of coeducation might not be hurt by any connection with woman suffrage. I now pledge my life insurance for the $2,000."

A few evenings later the Anthony parlor was crowded with people who had come to congratulate Susan. Girls who had been waiting to enter the University were there to express delight and appreciation. But Susan sat strangely silent and white-faced. Then she rose from her usual armchair and left the room.

Her sister Mary, who had been watching anxiously, excused herself and followed Susan upstairs. She found her lying on her bed, unconscious. It was a stroke, the beginning of the end.

Susan never fully recovered, although she lived on for a few more years. The first time she was well enough to go out, she wanted to be driven through the campus of the University. That night, with wavering letters, she wrote in her diary: "These are no longer forbidden grounds to the girls of our city. It is good to feel that the old doors swing on their hinges to admit them. Will the vows made to them be kept?"

JANE ADDAMS

"Love Thy Neighbor as Thyself"

1

Like many another young couple in 1844, Sarah and John Addams spent their honeymoon traveling westward in search of a new place to settle. When at last they saw the countryside of northern Illinois, with its beautiful sweep of open prairies and rolling hills, they knew they were home.

John Addams bought a gristmill on the edge of the Cedar River, in the village of Cedarville. Soon local farmers were coming to him with grain to be made into flour. As the years passed, the Addams family grew and prospered. Mr. Addams organized the building of a railroad into Cedarville. He became a banker, and a state senator. He was so highly respected that neighbors called him "the king gentle-man of the district."

The Addams' eighth child, Laura Jane, was born on September 6, 1860. She was a frail baby, but she survived. Two years later Mrs. Addams was again brought to bed with child. This time both mother and infant died.

Perhaps because the sickly little Jane had no mother, she grew up loving her father double. She followed him about like a small dog, and tried to imitate his ways and habits.

Mr. Addams was such a handsome, dignified man that Jane imagined all the strangers they ever met on the street or in the church were filled with admiration for him. Later she wrote, ". . . I prayed with all my heart that the ugly, pigeon-toed little girl, whose crooked back obliged her to walk with her head held very much upon one side, would never be pointed out to these visitors as the daughter of this fine man."

Now and then over the years, guests from outside Cedarville came to visit the Sunday School where Mr. Addams taught a Bible class. On such occasions, Jane tried to walk to church behind her father. In this way she hoped nobody would realize whose homely child she really was. She attached herself to her uncle James Addams. Uncle James would look down kindly and say, "So you are going to walk with me today?"

Maybe it wasn't fair to Uncle James to have this

ugly duckling by his side. Jane comforted herself
by thinking, "Anyway, his own little girl is not so
very pretty."

John Addams remarried when Jane was nearly
eight. This marriage gave her a stepbrother—George—
who was her own age. The two children had wonderful times playing around the handsome, ten-room
brick house Mr. Addams had built on a slope by
the Cedar River. One hill near the house was topped
with Norway pine trees, grown from seed Mr.
Addams had planted when he first came from
Pennsylvania in 1844. The millstream tumbled down
the sharp slope of another hill, which was almost
too steep to climb. There were enormous limestone
caves to explore, some of them thirty feet high. There
was a deserted kiln, where limestone and shells had
once been burned to make quicklime.

In addition to his flour mill, Mr. Addams now
owned a sawmill. Like a huge animal, the buzz saw
took sharp bites out of each log while it spewed
wood chips from its jagged teeth. Sometimes Jane
would sit on a log as it slowly approached those
jaws of noisy death. This was an exciting game: she
had to hop off at exactly the right moment, or risk
being cut in half!

The flour mill was nowhere near as stirring, but
Jane liked it better than the sawmill. Here there
were dusty corners for a girl to explore, and empty
bins for doll housekeeping. The basement was piled

with flours which were as good as sand to play with, especially when dampened with a little pot of river water.

Sometimes Mr. Addams went to town on business and permitted Jane to come along. Her father was president of the Second National Bank of Freeport, so they generally rode along the main street. Jane enjoyed the shops and the bustle. To the little country girl, a town of ten thousand people seemed a whirlpool of activity.

But one day Mr. Addams drove his horse and buggy to a mill, located in a part of town such as Jane had never imagined.

"These are horrid little houses, so close together!" she said.

"People do not live in ramshackle shanties by choice," said her father, "but only because it is the best they can do."

Jane's heart swelled with sympathy for these unfortunate people in their hideous homes. It looked as though the whole world had turned its back on them. "When I am grown up," she said, "I shall live in a large house, but it will not be built among other large houses. It will stand right among horrid little houses like these."

Jane and George loved it when their father reminisced about Abraham Lincoln. The two men had been friends when they worked together in the state government of Illinois. Mr. Addams greatly admired Lincoln for his sense of humor and his honesty, but above all for his views on democracy. For Mr. Addams objected to tyranny and injustice in any form, anywhere.

Sometimes Mr. Addams would go to his roll-top desk and take out a thin packet of Lincoln's letters. The children enjoyed looking over the letters, which all began, "My dear Double D'd Addams."

Their father often told them Lincoln anecdotes. One story was about a man who came up to Mr. Lincoln and said, "I'm the homeliest man in Stephenson County, Mr. Lincoln, and yet people tell me I look like you." To which Lincoln gravely replied, "Maybe so, maybe so. But I think I don't have quite so much cheek as you have."

Lincoln was fond of riddles, such as, "If you call a tail a leg, how many legs has a dog? Five? No, sir, calling a tail a leg don't *make* it a leg!"

Abraham Lincoln was elected President of the United States the year Jane was born, and she was only eight months old when the Civil War began. Later her father told her how he had helped organize and equip a company of soldiers called the "Addams Guard." His mill had worked day and night, grinding flour to make bread for the Union army.

One April day in 1865 Jane came home from play to find the white gateposts of her house draped in American flags and black cloth. She ran up the gravel walk and into her house. Her father told her Lincoln had been shot. "The greatest man in the world has died," he said, tears running down his

cheeks. Jane was astonished. She did not know that
grownups ever cried!

Besides discovering that grownups could cry, Jane
learned many other important things from her beloved father. Mr. Addams was a man who believed
that children, as part of the human race, are entitled to share in knowing what life is about. And he

discussed many serious matters with his daughter. "Is it right," he asked her, "to wear an especially elegant new cloak to Sunday School when you know it will make the other girls unhappy?"

And she was free to ask questions about matters that puzzled her. Such things as: "Why is it that some people are rich, while others have lives which are as hard as climbing a steep stairs?"

Or: "Why must some people eat their bread with tears?"

Or: "Is it true that everything that happens to a person is fated in advance?"

Mr. Addams treated Jane as though her child's mind was equal to his adult one, and this made a great impression on her. He did not know all the answers, and he told her so. He explained that the injustices of the world might never be straightened out, as far as clothes went, but there were many other things that mattered more than clothes. Everyone should have a chance to go to school, for instance. Also, people might differ in nationality, language, and beliefs, and yet they could "share large hopes and like desires" and work together to make their hopes come true. From her father, Jane learned that "the things that make us alike are stronger than the things that make us different."

"Above all," said Mr. Addams, "always be honest with yourself inside, whatever happens. It is very important not to pretend to understand what you don't understand."

There was one thing Jane did not understand: Did her father *really* like her, such a plain Jane with a crooked back? She would think then of the long walks and talks and rides she and her father enjoyed together, and would decide it was a foolish worry. But again that black ghost rose to haunt her: Maybe her handsome father was secretly ashamed? Maybe he hated to admit to strangers that this girl was his?

One afternoon as Jane was walking down the busy main street of Freeport, she saw her father coming out of the bank. Jane held her breath. The street was full of strangers. Nobody knew who she was, so her father was quite safe. He could pretend he had never seen this girl before. Just then Mr. Addams noticed Jane in the crowd. Raising his high silk hat, he singled out his daughter with a delighted smile and an especially courtly bow. Jane's ghost of fear crumpled and disappeared forever.

When Jane was seventeen she went to a boarding school, the Rockford Seminary. The school was a simple, hard-working establishment where the students all cleaned their own rooms and did their own chores. Jane studied the subjects that were offered to young ladies of her day—mental and moral philosophy, natural science, ancient history and literature, ancient languages. She and her classmates had endless discussions about what they would do when they finished school. Many of the girls talked about becoming missionaries so they could carry their religious beliefs and their good works to the people of other lands. They tried to persuade Jane to do the same, but she clung stubbornly to her own ideas. She wanted to become a doctor and "live with the poor."

The summer after Jane finished school, she and George were with their parents on a pleasant trip to Lake Superior when Mr. Addams suddenly fell ill and died.

Messages of condolence poured in from all over the state. An editor of the Chicago *Times* wrote, "I know of many men who have never accepted a bribe. But I can testify that John Addams was never even *offered* one. Bad men kept out of his way by instinct."

Her father's death was a stunning blow to the twenty-one-year-old Jane, and she struggled in vain to recover her good spirits. One sad August day, that year of 1881, a sympathetic friend took the grieving girl out for a walk. Professor Blaisdell and the young woman slowly climbed a hilltop. They stood looking down at the familiar lanes and chimneys of the little village of Cedarville. Suddenly Jane understood that her own grief was the tiniest drop in the "torrent of sorrow which flows under the footsteps of man." All God's creatures meet trouble. Every human being faces death. But it is only in

the companionship of shared experiences that people,
by helping one another, comfort themselves.

Jane went to Philadelphia and spent the next
winter studying at Woman's Medical College. Then
her old spinal ailment returned. She had an operation and spent six months in bed. This straightened
her back but left her in a state of nerves.

Her doctor recommended that she give up all
idea of practicing medicine, and travel in Europe
for a year or two. "Visit the art galleries. Go to the
opera," he said. "Take advantage of your position
in life, and enjoy yourself!"

Poor Jane! She was not poor in the usual sense, because she had plenty of money with which to travel
and enjoy herself. She was poor because her spirit was
restless. She hated to feel useless. She could not
bear to look forward to a lifetime of being a well-

bred lady of the nineteenth century, sitting in the parlor with book or embroidery or a graceful song at the pianoforte while real life passed her by. *Somebody* must need her!

But she did not yet know who it could be, or what, or where. So in 1883 Jane set forth on the first of her many trips to Europe. Her little party of eight sailed first to Ireland, visited Scotland, and then traveled down to London where they went eagerly about, taking in the sights.

The London of that day was a fast-growing industrial city, tumbling with hordes of people who flowed in from the countryside to fill the constantly increasing need for labor. Hundreds of factory workers earned starvation wages. Many hundreds of others, like uprooted plants, could not find any nourishment in the stony soil of city life. All these people crowded into the poorest neighborhoods and lived a catch-as-catch-can existence.

Wherever Jane traveled, she saw stately buildings and beautiful gardens, but she also saw misery, "hideous human need and suffering." One Saturday evening a London missionary took the small party of tourists on a sightseeing trip. They rode to a slum district in London's East End to watch a fruit and vegetable auction. These foods were leftovers from the regular market. Since they were wilted and spoiling and could not be sold any other way, they were auctioned off to the poor.

Crowds of tattered people swarmed around the

carts where hucksters were scornfully tossing out rotting vegetables to the highest bidder. Jane saw one wretch catch a head of cabbage. The cabbage was raw and filthy, the man was ragged and unwashed. He sat down on the curb and tore into that cabbage with tooth and claw, devouring it like an animal.

Jane was horrified. As her party drove away from the scene, she was left with a vivid picture: ". . . the final impression was not of ragged, tawdry clothing nor of pinched and sallow faces, but of myriads of hands, empty, pathetic, nerveless and workworn, showing white in the uncertain light of the street, and clutching forward for food which was already unfit to eat."

In the next half-dozen years Jane traveled widely. But whether she was in one of the great cities of the United States or a tourist in France, Germany, Spain, or Italy, everywhere it was the same. On the one hand she saw well-dressed families walking proudly along paths of comfort and beauty. On the other hand, cities were filled with tattered wretches bent double by the weight of heavy lives.

During the restless 1880s, this spectacle of social injustice moved a handful of other people to right wrongs and relieve suffering. In 1884 an English churchman, Canon Samuel Barnett, opened a residence in London's dreadful East End. Here university lads from Oxford and Cambridge came to live and share their ideals of neighborliness and citizen-

ship with others in the slum. This residence, named
Toynbee Hall, was called a "settlement" because the
students "settled" here and formed a neighborhood
center.

A purpose which had been a long time growing
in Jane blossomed at last. She would open a settle-

ment house in Chicago and be a neighbor to the
poor. Any of her educated friends who agreed that
democracy must be lived through action could come
live and work with her. Rich and poor together
would "learn of life from life itself."

In June, 1888, Jane returned to London. She visited Toynbee Hall and learned all she could about running a settlement. Then she went to Chicago to find her "big house among the poor."

For months Miss Addams scoured Chicago looking for a likely place to settle. She talked with truant officers, missionaries, architects, newspaper reporters—anybody who might lead her to a suitable location. No luck. Then one Sunday afternoon in early spring, while riding in a friend's carriage, Miss Addams spotted a fine old house standing graciously among the tenements. On one side stood an undertaker's establishment; on the other side, a saloon. The house was of brick, two stories high, framed by a friendly porch with beautifully carved wooden pillars.

But before Miss Addams could note its exact location, her host's carriage whipped past the house, turned a corner, and the place passed from view. Next day Miss Addams went back to the neighborhood on foot. She searched up and down the blocks for several days before she had to give up. The house was lost!

Three weeks later she decided to accept the advice of friends who had lived in Chicago all their lives and knew it inside out. They drew a circle on a map to show her that the proposed settlement should be located somewhere in the neighborhood of Blue Island Avenue, Halsted Street, and Harrison Street. This was the very center of Chicago's foreign quarter. The tens of thousands of people who struggled for existence here had come from all over Europe. There were Italians from Naples, Sicily, and Calabria; Jews from Poland, Russia, and Bohemia; French Canadians, Irishmen, Germans, Greeks, Dutch, Scotch, Scandinavians. There were also first-generation Americans, children of these foreign born. In the great "melting pot" of America, most of these nationality groups were not yet melted. Such people held fearfully to old, familiar ways of life and quarreled with neighbors who spoke in other tongues.

Again Miss Addams began her search. Imagine her joy when, at the corner of Halsted and Polk streets, she came upon the hospitable old house she had glimpsed earlier! It certainly had seen better days in the thirty-three years since Mr. Charles Hull built it for his family. The Hulls were long since gone. Now part of the run-down house was used for offices and a factory storehouse. People still lived on the second floor, in spite of the rumor that the attic was haunted. To play safe, the tenants kept a filled pitcher standing ready on the stairs that led to the attic. They understood that ghosts could not cross water.

Gracious old Hull-House rose like an island in a sea of three- and four-story tenements. Halsted Street and the alleys around it were narrow and crowded. The streets were paved with squares of wood. Here and there people had pried out these cedarwood paving blocks to burn for firewood, leaving dangerous holes. The streets were unbelievably dirty

and evil-smelling, with rotting garbage and ashes overflowing from wooden boxes fastened to the pavement. Of course the city had laws about cleaning the streets and collecting the garbage—but un-

fortunately nobody was doing much about enforcing
them.

Crooked little unlighted alleys crisscrossed the
main thoroughfares of the neighborhood. These back

alleys also were crammed with tenements. A few houses were made of brick, but mostly they were of wood. Not many had fire escapes, and almost none of them had inside water. In the back yard there was usually a faucet that served all the people in all the apartments in the house. Miss Addams met an old German woman who had spent the last four years carrying water up and down two flights of stairs, seven days a week, so she could wash the heavy flannel suits of men who worked in an iron foundry. Her pay? Thirty-five cents a day.

The city of Chicago had a public sewer system, but many of the tenements were not connected with it. People used outhouses, often filthy and dilapidated. The stench from these outdoor, open toilets was unbelievable. And, within a circle one-third of a square mile around Hull-House, there were only three bathtubs!

Of course the landlords of these tenement houses made more money from their rents when they did not have to supply such services as running water and sewer systems. They complained that there was no point in fixing up their houses anyway, because foreign tenants did not know how to live properly in a modern city. If such people were given a bathtub, they would use it to store coal.

It was true that simple country people frequently tried to carry on their usual activities in their usual way, even when the usual way was not suitable any more. For example, the Greek peasants continued their time-honored custom of slaughtering sheep—but did it in tenement basements. People baked bread for their neighbors—but in unspeakably filthy quarters. One Italian artist carved on the doorposts of his tenement the same pattern he had used on an altar screen in his church in Naples. Was his landlord happy with this beautiful new decoration? He was not! He accused the tenant of destroying private property, and put him out.

Factories, offices, warehouses, and shops were crammed among the dwelling houses of the neighborhood. To the south of Hull-House were the foul-smelling Chicago stockyards; to the north were ship-building yards. In between there were butcher shops and groceries, saloons and dance halls, clothing stores and pawn shops. Hawkers with pushcarts stood at the curb, selling every sort of vegetable and fruit, household article and item of clothing. Tucked into dark basements, smelly stable lofts, rear shanties and back tenement rooms, people toiled to make glass, or boxes, or cigars, or candy, or clothing.

In those days there were no laws to say how long a man should work, or how much he must be paid. There was no provision for him if he was ill or out of work. If a man came down with pneumonia from digging ditches in the rain, or if he got tuberculosis after years of breathing lint in a textile factory, or if he lost an arm in a piece of moving machinery— too bad for him. There were plenty of others willing and able to take his place.

Common laborers worked twelve and fourteen hours a day to earn about ten dollars a week. Often their wives and children worked too for whatever they could add to the skimpy household income.

Employers liked to hire children. They were quick and nimble, and because they were children they could be paid less than grown people. In the sewing trades, children made about four cents an hour. Even a youngster of five could sit by her mother, hour after weary hour, pulling out basting threads. Older girls ran errands, or pasted labels on jars, or sorted rags, or worked in a candy factory. When Miss Addams offered Christmas candy to a group of girls, the little ones turned away. They worked with candy from seven in the morning until nine in the evening and "could not bear the sight of it."

Boys delivered packages, collected scrap iron, worked in glass factories or laundries, or sold papers on the street to earn perhaps three dollars a week. Children were often injured or killed at their jobs. A few dollars would have bought a safeguard for a piece of open machinery, but most often an employer did not spend money to protect children. Instead, parents signed a legal paper promising that they would never claim damages if their child was "careless" and injured himself while working.

This, then, was the neighborhood where Jane Addams wanted to live and work.

3

At last, on September 18, 1889, Jane Addams, her friend Ellen Starr, and their housekeeper Mary Keyser moved into Hull-House. Now they would simply see what needed to be done, and do it! That first night the young women were so excited they forgot to lock the street door.

Nobody broke in, but in the following days many people came. First, perhaps, they came shyly and out of curiosity; or boldly, to see what was in it for them. Soon there were two thousand people a week streaming in and out of Hull-House from early morning to late at night. Men, women, and children came to reading clubs, discussion groups, kindergarten, dramatics, sports, concerts, cooking lessons, sewing circles, classes in English and citizenship. They enjoyed social clubs, an art gallery, a branch room of the Chicago public library. There was even a branch post office in Hull-House so people could mail their precious letters directly to Europe. Otherwise, shrewd swindlers offered to help them send money to relatives back home and then took advantage of the immigrants' ignorance to cheat them cruelly.

Many came for help with their troubles. A woman's husband had walked out after a quarrel and never returned home. Now how would she feed the children? A man had died, and his bewildered widow did not know how to go about collecting his insurance. An old lady was losing her mind. Her daughter could not care for her at home any longer. But where should she send her mother? How could she convince the frightened old lady that she would still be safe and looked after? A baby was born with a deformed face, and his mother refused to keep him. A fifteen-year-old bride was afraid of her husband. He beat her up every night because she had lost her wedding ring.

Miss Addams and Miss Starr were joined by other friends who came to live and work at Hull-House, and by volunteers who came from all over the city to give as many hours of time as they could spare. The first years passed in a whirl of activity and a blur of fatigue. Miss Addams kept a careful budget and worried about unpaid bills. The Hull-House residents pitched in to cook meals and wash windows. They scrimped and saved for projects dear to their hearts. There were so many things that needed doing, large and small . . .

People came to love friendly Miss Addams. Often she stopped a neighbor on the street to admire her new baby or ask if Hull-House could borrow her beautifully hand-woven shawl. Hull-House had a labor museum to show how weaving was done in the different countries of Europe.

During social affairs held at the settlement house, people met their neighbors and enjoyed a recess from their own dreary rooms. Hull-House was a pleasant place, furnished with paintings and art objects.

On one occasion an Italian housewife saw a vase of red roses and greeted them like long-lost friends.

"Can it be! Fresh roses from my country!" she said.

"Oh, no," said Miss Addams. "These roses came from a florist's shop not ten blocks from where you live."

"It is not possible," insisted the foreign-born woman in her broken English. "I live in Chicago for six years and I never see the roses. There are in Italy in the summer many, many flowers."

The big projects at Hull-House grew naturally from the neighborhood's urgent needs. For instance, many women worked in the garment industry, in places called "sweatshops" because their employers required long hours at low wages under poor working conditions. After a woman had sewed steadily for twelve hours in a typical sweatshop, she had little energy left for shopping and cooking for her family. At mealtime she would either open a few cans, or perhaps give her children some pennies and tell them to fend for themselves. The children would proceed to eat their dinner at the nearest candy store.

When mothers went out to work, there was no one at home to look after the small children. Sometimes a neighbor would "keep an eye out," but more often a mother had no choice but to lock her youngsters in the tenement rooms. An infant tied to a table leg or the side of his crib, day after day, month after month, could not grow normally. And if a child did not become crippled from being tied, there was a good chance he would kill or injure himself playing with matches, or tumbling out of a window.

In the summertime, mothers faced a different problem. They did not dare to leave toddlers tied in unbearably hot rooms. But there were so many sneak thieves around that they did not dare leave the doors open, either. So they would give each child a penny for something to eat, and lock him out of the apartment. These mites then spent their days roaming the neighborhood, playing in the streets, hunting for scraps in the garbage boxes, searching for cool hallways to rest in.

Understandably, one of Hull-House's first projects was a kindergarten, and soon afterward a day nursery where working mothers could leave their children. Another project was a public kitchen, where people could buy nourishing soups and stews at low price.

At first people hung back from buying meals at the public kitchens. They were not sure they liked strange American food. An Irishwoman grudgingly admitted the soups were nourishing, but she wanted to eat "what she'd ruther." An Italian was surprised to discover how many different things Americans ate. He lived next door to a saloon, and had never seen the customers there consume anything but the potatoes and beer sold there.

Even in the kindergarten, children began by being unfriendly to those who were different from themselves. "*We* eat spaghetti this way!" said one Italian tot to Jennie Dow, the kindergarten teacher. He showed her how to wind spaghetti neatly around a fork. Then he pointed in disgust to Angelina, who was happily bending back her head and allowing a waterfall of spaghetti to flow into her mouth from above. "Angelina's way is wrong," said Tony, "and I won't sit next to *her!*"

The lack of bathtubs in the neighborhood troubled Miss Addams. Three tubs were installed in the basement of Hull-House. These were in constant use by people of the neighborhood while Miss Addams badgered the Chicago Board of Health for more facilities. At last, after several years, the authorities grudgingly agreed to build a public bathhouse on a lot belonging to a friend of Hull-House. The officials complained that nobody would use these baths; they were simply wasting ten thousand dollars of public money. When the baths were opened, however, they were such an immediate and overflowing success that Chicago went ahead and built others.

Another cause for distress was the wretched housing. Hull-House workers began to give public talks about the need for housing reform. One young man who owned a block of tenements grew so ashamed of his property that he gave it to Hull-House. Miss

Addams found the tenements too decayed to improve, so she tore them down and used the land for a badly needed playground. After this, playgrounds and small parks began to spring up in other city areas.

Miss Addams worried about the overflowing, festering garbage boxes that lined the streets of Chicago's nineteenth ward, a district where fifty thousand people lived. These garbage boxes, swarming with rats and flies, were hideous to see. They created sickening odors. But worst of all, the vermin brought sickness and death into the tenements. People called such ailments "filth-disease."

At Hull-House there was a small incinerator for burning garbage. Miss Addams and Dr. Alice Hamilton, a Hull-House resident, gave many talks to the immigrant women. "In your native village it is all right to sweep your own doorway and let the refuse decay in open air and sunshine," they would tell the women. "But here in the city, if garbage is not collected and destroyed, you will see your children sicken and die. It is not enough to keep your own houses clean. You must also insist that the authorities keep the city clean."

Over and over again, Miss Addams complained to City Hall that the garbage was not being collected properly. Nothing happened. In each ward there was a city-appointed garbage inspector. The job was called a political "plum" because it paid a salary of one thousand dollars a year and required little work in return. The inspector accepted his appointment, pocketed his salary, and minded his own business while the garbage contractor minded his. If a contractor was paid to use thirteen wagons to collect garbage every day, but instead used five wagons and didn't get around every day—well, naturally, his expenses went down and his profits went up.

Four years of complaining to City Hall got Miss Addams nowhere. Then she asked for help from the energetic members of the Hull-House Woman's Club. Three times a week, during the sizzling evenings of July and August, twelve determined women tramped up and down dirty streets and dim alleys, inspecting the condition of their neighbors' garbage boxes, and noting violations. Hull-House reported each violation of the law to the health department at City Hall: one thousand and thirty-seven of them!

In rapid order, three garbage inspectors were transferred in and then out of the nineteenth ward. But the death rate remained high and the garbage situation did not improve. In desperation, Jane Addams decided she would collect the garbage herself. With the help of two business friends, she put in a bid with the city for the job of garbage removal, nineteenth ward. She did not receive the job. Instead, the mayor appointed her garbage inspector of the nineteenth ward—the only paid job she ever held in her life!

Every morning, rain or shine, Miss Addams left Hull-House at six o'clock to follow the garbage col-

lectors at their work. She saw to it that they really emptied every box, and that they took their loads all the way to the dump instead of dropping them somewhere along the street. She insisted that the contractor increase the number of wagons he used— from nine to thirteen, then from thirteen to seventeen. She insisted that he remove the bodies of dead horses from the streets, as he was well paid to do, instead of leaving them until a police ambulance finally carted them off. The garbage contractor moaned and groaned and claimed he would die in the poorhouse.

In one alley, Miss Addams got some neighborhood boys to help her shovel garbage off the street. After they had scraped eight inches down and still did not strike bottom, Miss Addams insisted that Chicago's street commissioner take over the work. He did. The carpet of garbage proved to be eighteen inches thick, with cedar-block paving at the bottom.

At about this time, Miss Addams' job of inspector was taken over by Amanda Johnson, a trained co-worker. To the great joy of many citizens, the work was taken out of politics in 1895, when the state government of Illinois made it a civil service job.

One important lesson Jane Addams learned was that a few individuals, working alone, could not hope to stem the flow of the "torrent of misery." It was too vast. And just as people living side by side worked together to make their neighborhood a cleaner place in which to live, so Hull-House residents found themselves working with people of other groups to bring about much-needed reforms.

Miss Addams was deeply interested in the welfare of children, and eager for a law to improve the hours and conditions of their work. In her usual way, she set about getting the facts. She and a co-worker, Florence Kelley, visited hundreds of factories and sweatshops and collected masses of facts. Hull-House turned these industrial statistics over to the Illinois State Bureau of Labor. At the same time, Miss Addams traveled endlessly in the city and the state. She talked to members of women's clubs, religious groups and trade unions, urging them to join the fight.

She stirred up a lot of opposition. Old ways of thinking die hard, and many people of that day resented the way women were taking part in public affairs. "It is not Jane Addams' job to lobby for a law any more than it is decent for her to go around collecting garbage," said the die-hards. "A woman's place is in the home."

Bitter objections came, too, from some parents of working children.

"I'm unemployed," said one father, "but my Flo has a job in a glass factory and Jelly sells newspapers on the street. Without the money they give me, how will I live? Besides, the kids don't want to go to school. They'd much rather work."

But by far the biggest storm came from factory owners who thought that government regulations meant ruin to them. Their own hard work, they said, had made America a booming land. Labor was a natural resource, like the iron, coal, oil, and timber they used so freely. Government control, they said, was the work of radicals who wanted to put them out of business. Trade unions, which were organizations of workers, were radical. Jane Addams, who encouraged trade unions, was radical.

One day two wealthy men took Miss Addams to lunch in an expensive club. "We are speaking for a group of factory owners," they told her. "Drop this radical nonsense about a sweatshop bill and we will

give you a donation of fifty thousand dollars to use
in your other activities. Hull-House could become
the largest institution on the West Side!"

In those days, fifty thousand dollars was an
enormous sum. And it was a fact that at Hull-House
money disappeared like water into sand. But Miss
Addams remembered the *Times* editorial about her
incorruptible father, and she flushed with shame.
What weakness did they see in her, she wondered,
that these men dared so much as approach John
Addams' daughter with a bribe?

Controlling her anger, Miss Addams quietly explained to her luncheon hosts that it was not her
ambition to make Hull-House the largest institution
on the West Side. "Our concern is to protect our
neighbors from poor conditions of work," she said.
"If destroying Hull-House could do this, then we
would cheerfully destroy Hull-House.

"And," she added, "sing a *Te Deum* on its ruins!"

The child-labor bill became law in Illinois on July
1, 1903.

In this way, working calmly but steadily toward
the changes she saw were needed, Jane Addams
helped bring about many laws to establish a better
social order: an eight-hour working day, minimum
wages, industrial safeguards, sickness and unemploy-
ment insurance, special courts for children in trouble
with the law, votes for women. The activities at
Hull-House became models for hundreds of other
settlements throughout the world.

In her later years Miss Addams spent most of her time in the cause of disarmament and world peace. She never outgrew her belief that nations, like the people of many nationalities in her beloved Hull-House neighborhood, could learn to live together in peace and settle their differences in honest discussion.

Even during World War I, when it was very unpopular to talk about peace, Jane Addams traveled the world over, writing and talking about peace. In 1915 she became the first president of a new world organization which came to be called the Women's International League for Peace and Freedom.

In December, 1931, Miss Addams was awarded the Nobel Peace Prize. She was in the hospital waiting to have a serious operation when she learned she would share the $30,000 prize money with Dr. Nicholas Murray Butler, president of Columbia University. Characteristically, Miss Addams gave her part of the money to the Women's International League to carry on the struggle for peace and freedom.

Though the years that followed brought failing health, Miss Addams kept right on fighting for her beliefs. At a dinner in her honor the ailing elderly lady heard a member of President Franklin D. Roosevelt's cabinet pay this well-earned tribute:

Parents who want to develop the finest in their children will bring them up in the Jane Addams

*tradition and those so reared will be the best
citizens of their generation—steadfast, neighborly,
serene and simple, crusaders in the never-ending
fight for a finer and better social order . . .*

When she died in Chicago on May 21, 1935, this
woman who believed in "love thy neighbor as thyself" had thousands of friends the world over. From
world dignitaries to plain nineteenth ward neighbors,
they jammed Hull-House to attend a simple funeral
service. And then the body of Jane Addams was
returned to the old cemetery in Cedarville and
placed near the grave of her beloved father.

MARY McLEOD BETHUNE

"Walk Proudly in the Light!"

1

Six-year-old Mary Jane McLeod and her mother
Patsy walked along the dusty road carrying a basket
of freshly ironed clothes between them. A September
sun shone on the child's tight black braids and on
her broad, almost purple-black little face. The country
air near Mayesville, South Carolina, rocked to the
lusty tones of the spiritual Mary was singing:

> *When Israel was in Egypt land,*
> *Let my people go.*
> *Oppressed so hard they could not stand,*
> *Let my people go . . .*

But as they came near the big white mansion belonging to Mr. Ben Wilson, Mary fell silent. Her mother had once been a Wilson slave. Mary felt cautious about white people. One had to be very careful, and the best thing was to keep out of their way whenever possible.

While her mother carried the laundry in at the back entrance, Mary waited outdoors. Off to one side of the lawn was a playhouse, in perfect imitation of a mansion. Around the playhouse, various toys lay scattered about.

Mary's eyes took in a striped ball, a rocking horse, and some dolls sitting at a tiny tea table. They came to rest on a book tossed near the base of a live-oak tree.

Mary was fascinated by books. In her family's cabin there was one book. It was a Bible, which her mother respectfully kept on a special shelf. But neither her grandmother, her father, her mother, her sixteen brothers and sisters nor Mary herself could understand the mystery of the black marks that neatly lined every page.

Mary squatted under the live-oak tree and picked up the book. She opened it to a page with a picture of an apple.

One of the Wilson granddaughters popped out of the playhouse. Mary, carried away with desire, did a rash thing. She pointed to the letter "A" printed under the apple and asked, "Please, what does it spell?"

This was the year 1881. The Civil War had been fought and won. Negroes had been legally free since December 18, 1865, when the Thirteenth Amendment was added to the Constitution. But most white Southerners were still afraid of what would happen if Negroes were really free. So they were fighting another kind of war, a bitter battle to keep the Negroes in an inferior position. If a people are uneducated, unable to know their rights or hold good jobs or speak through their government, then they are still enslaved even though they are not legally slaves.

Little Miss Wilson, like other white children, had been carefully taught that "all men are created equal, except Negroes." Thus it was natural for her to rush over to the Negro child, snatch the book away, and say scornfully, "You can't read! You're black!"

Trudging home beside her mother, Mary said from the depths of her heart, "I want to learn to read. I crave it for all us people."

Patsy McLeod shook her head and sighed. Of course there were always a few Negroes who managed to obtain an education, but it was not likely that Mary would be one of them. Not a single grown-up Negro in Mayesville, South Carolina, could read.

"We have no teacher, child, and we have no school," said Patsy to her daughter. "You know that."

Mary was the fifteenth of Patsy and Sam McLeod's seventeen children. From the beginning she was different from the others. "This child has a rising soul," Patsy said to Sam while Mary was still an infant. "She will either go far or break her heart."

How was she different? Before Mary Jane McLeod was even born, Abraham Lincoln said something that described her nature: "It is difficult to make a man miserable while he feels he is worthy of himself and claims kindred to the great God who made him."

But on this lovely Saturday afternoon when Patsy McLeod shook her head so sadly, Mary had no inkling that her life would be a key that opened doors for the Negroes of America. She just said to her mother, "Then the teacher and the school will come. The Lord will send them."

Mary's people were descendants of Africans who had been captured by white traders and carried off their native soil to lives of slavery in the New World. Her father, Sam (slaves did not have last names), was a field hand on the McLeod plantation in South Carolina. Patsy, her mother, belonged to the nearby estate of Mr. Wilson, just outside the tiny town of Mayesville.

Patsy and Sam met one day when Sam was delivering a message from Mr. McLeod to Mr. Wilson. The young couple quickly fell in love and wanted to get married. In the days before the Civil War, however, slaves were legally not supposed to marry. Some couples did manage to get married, but when the man and the woman belonged to different masters it was especially difficult.

Just the same, Sam took his courage in hand and spoke of his hopes to Mr. McLeod. His master might have laughed, but he didn't.

"Tell you what, Sam," he said. "If Mr. Wilson agrees to sell Patsy, I'll let you earn money and pay for her."

Mr. Wilson proved willing, and set a price on Patsy. Sam left the cotton fields and began to work at a lumber mill. Six days a week he walked three miles to the mill, worked fourteen hours, and then walked three miles back again. In two years he earned enough money to buy his future wife.

Now Patsy was free—or did she belong to Sam? Neither. Now she was simply a McLeod slave instead of a Wilson slave.

But they could get married! Mrs. Wilson kindly gave Patsy one of her castoff party dresses, and at Christmas time Patsy and Sam had a real wedding in the Wilson parlor. Then they walked back to the McLeod slave quarters and, the next day, continued their lives of work in the cotton fields.

This went on for many years. Whenever Patsy had a baby she was given a few days off. Then she would return to the crop with the newest baby tied to her back, or resting near by in the shade. Almost as soon as a child could walk he, too, went to work spading earth, hoeing and chopping weeds, and picking cotton. Patsy and Sam did not complain. Mr. McLeod was a kind master. He did not beat his slaves, and he did not sell any of their children.

In 1861 the Civil War began. Plantation owners left home to fight in the Confederate Army for their right to withdraw from the Union on the question of slavery. The slaves worked on more or less as usual during the next year or two while they pieced together bits of information from overheard conversations, gossip, passing strangers . . .

Then the grapevine brought them news of President Lincoln's Emancipation Proclamation of January 1, 1863: The slaves were free! Patsy's old mother, Sophia, was still living on the Wilson plantation. She packed her few belongings that very night, and walked over to join her daughter's family in their dirt-floor cabin at the McLeods'.

Many McLeod slaves promptly walked off the plantation, but not Patsy and Sam. Where would they go? How would they find food and a place out of the rain for themselves, ten children, and grandmother Sophia? Freedom took planning.

Mr. McLeod returned from the war. "You can stay on here if you like," he said. "I'll feed you and pay you something if I can, in exchange for your work."

While Sam worked for Mr. McLeod, Patsy did laundering and cleaning for Mrs. Wilson. Patsy and Sam had their hearts set on buying a piece of good cotton-growing South Carolina land, and Mr. Wilson agreed to sell them some.

It took more than four years, but one proud day in 1870 Sam walked to the county courthouse to register a piece of paper that proved he owned five acres of land.

"Last name?" asked the courthouse clerk.

"Just Sam, that's all the name I have."

"You've got to give me a surname, or the deed isn't legal," said the clerk.

Sam scratched his head. After a moment's thought, he borrowed a familiar name. "Put me down as Sam McLeod," he said.

Over the next two years, in their spare time, Sam McLeod and his sons cleared land, split logs, and built a three-room cabin. They floored it with warped boards the lumber mill gave them, and fashioned a fireplace with clay from the swamp. Meanwhile, Patsy continued to work in the Wilson kitchen, and her wages supplied an ornery old mule, a rickety wagon, and a plow.

Not an elaborate house, surely. It had a fireplace for a cook stove, and straw-filled sacks for beds. There was a plank for a kitchen table, with only enough room for half the family to eat at a time. But it was their home and their land, and they were filled with self-respect and hope. Some years, when they were lucky, they could even afford such luxuries as sugar for the coffee and tobacco for Grandma Sophia's corncob pipe.

When Mary Jane McLeod came along in July, 1875, she was the first of their children born into the freedom of their very own home. Maybe that is why they felt she was different.

Mary grew into a strong, husky girl. Like the other McLeod children she worked in the fields from dawn to sunset. By the time she was nine, she could pick 250 pounds of cotton a day. When the mule was sick, she could put the traces over her own young shoulders and pull that plow herself.

It was a life of endless work, and it seemed to stretch just as endlessly into the future. But Mary dreamed. Years afterward she said, "As a child, working in the cotton fields, I had a vision in which I saw buildings and wide-open doors and people finding themselves welcome inside. I believed it would come to pass. For I had faith in me. Like a deep river."

When she was eleven, Mary's faith came to pass. The Mission Board of the northern branch of the Presbyterian Church opened a school for Negro children in Mayesville.

"Rise and shine and give God the glory!" sang Mary as she picked the fluffy cotton bolls and stuffed them into her burlap sack. But then she began to worry. Some of her older brothers and sisters were gone from the household now, working elsewhere as cooks, stablemen, day laborers. Could her parents spare her?

Mary's father and mother were poor, ignorant people. They had no book learning, but they had deep springs of natural understanding. "Yes, we can spare Mary," they said. "This child is going to walk with her head up!"

Mary had to finish the season's work, so school was a few weeks along before that magical first morning when she took her place on a row of benches in the unpainted two-room wooden building near the railroad tracks. The teacher was a neatly dressed young Negro woman and her name was Miss Emma Wilson. The "Miss" made a powerful impression on Mary. She had never before heard any Negro—man or woman—addressed with a title of respect.

The school term lasted only four months, but Mary absorbed learning the way a dry sponge picks up water. As soon as the miracle of the alphabet was clear to her, she began to explain it to her brothers and sisters at home. As soon as she understood the marvel of numbers, her father and his neighbors came to her with questions.

"How do I figure the weight of a bale of cotton?"

"What is my percentage of this year's crop?"

"Is this bill from the general store added up honestly?"

These people had been cheated and short-changed all their lives because they could not protect themselves with simple arithmetic.

By 1889, when Mary was fourteen, she had taken every subject Miss Wilson offered. And that summer the family suffered a crushing blow: the mule died. Mary thought she would have to give up her dream of further schooling and become, instead, the family's mule.

But fate spun a different thread. In faraway Denver, Colorado, lived a quiet little spinster named Mary Crissman. Miss Crissman was a Quaker whose religion said that no human being is better than another simply by accident of color. She was distressed by the condition of Negroes in the South. She saw that chains of ignorance could be as heavy as chains of steel.

Miss Crissman decided she could help, in a tiny way. She sat down at her desk and wrote a letter to Mr. Satterfield, principal of the Scotia Seminary in Concord, North Carolina. She explained that she followed her religion in always setting aside ten cents out of each dollar she earned to use as a "tithe" in helping others. Her income as a seamstress was not large, said Miss Crissman, but she hoped her tithe might be enough to pay for the education of one Negro girl. Please, said Miss Crissman, select "one you are sure will make good."

It happened that Miss Emma Wilson was staying at the Scotia Seminary when Miss Crissman's letter to Mr. Satterfield arrived. And so, when Miss Wilson returned to Mayesville a few weeks later to reopen her own school, she hurried out to the McLeod place.

"Mary has a scholarship!" she told the delighted family. "Here's a letter to prove it, and a railway ticket to Concord. You must get her ready at once. She'll need clothes and a pair of shoes. She can't wear flour-sack dresses and walk barefoot in Concord!"

Mary's father borrowed money from the bank and bought another mule. Mary and her mother and grandmother sat up late, night after night, sewing and singing. It was a time for rejoicing.

When the great day came, a crowd of neighbors gathered at the railway station to see Mary off on an eight-hour ride that would take her into another world. Mary's clothes were wrapped in paper bundles and she carried a fried-chicken lunch. Her heavy new shoes squeaked and her heart was bursting. She ached to go, but she also ached to lose her family. How would she keep in touch with these people she loved, when they could not write to her nor read her letters to them?

Miss Wilson sensed Mary's struggle. She put an

arm around the girl's shoulders and whispered,
"Write your news to me. I'll read the letters aloud."

So it was through Mary's letters to her first teacher
that her family learned about life at Scotia. Her
room was on the top floor of a very high building,
wrote Mary—four stories high! It was called Faith
Hall, a wonderful name. Mary shared a room with
Abby Greeley. Just think, only two people using a
whole room! There were real beds and mattresses in
it, and a washstand. There were pictures on the wall.

Everybody ate together in a large dining hall
downstairs. The long table had a white cloth on it,
and vases of flowers. Each person had his own knife,
fork, and spoon. The silverware gave Mary a little
trouble at first. Finally she confessed to one of the
teachers, "You'll have to show me, ma'am. In Mayesville forks are just for white folks!"

Much later in life, Mary looked back at her Scotia
Seminary days and described what was most important of all. Some of the Scotia teachers were
white, as was the principal, but they worked and ate
and sang side by side with Negro teachers and
students. "The white teachers taught that the color
of a person's skin has nothing to do with his brains,"
Mary wrote, "and that color, caste, or class distinc-
tions are an evil thing . . ." Mary lost her fear of
white folk.

During school hours she studied English, Latin,
mathematics, and science. After school and during
holidays she worked in the laundry and kitchen.

Mary was proud of her work. Later she wrote, "The stairs were always beautiful. The supervisor always gave me good marks on cleaning and scrubbing and dusting and cooking. I realized that I had to do it well, because I was laying the foundation for a real life."

Mary was able to visit home only twice during the years at Scotia. The second time was just after graduation, the summer before she went to Chicago to study at the Moody Bible Institute. At this time in her life, Mary wanted to become a missionary in Africa.

The young lady who boarded the train going to Chicago was a very different person from the girl who first left Mayesville for Concord. But prejudice against Negroes had not changed. When Mary started up the steps of the red-plush day coach the conductor stopped her. "Colored coach is up front by the engine," he told her. He surveyed her neatly dressed figure, her straw hat, her suitcase. "My, some of you niggers is sure gittin' uppity," he said.

Mary walked up front to the made-over baggage car with wooden benches. The air was heavy with a smell of unwashed bodies and unswept floors. Ahead of her, a white-haired old woman fumbled up the aisle. "Move along, you black cow!" roared the conductor.

At Moody Bible Institute, Mary was the only Negro student. "White people's eyes pierced me," she wrote. "Some of them were kind eyes; others would like to be but were still afraid."

The weeks in Chicago went by in Bible study, choir practice, and field service. Field service meant talking with prisoners in jail, offering help to drunkards and beggars, praying with sinners. Mary visited Hull-House, too, and admired what Jane Addams was doing for the people of her neighborhood. When she was a missionary, Mary thought, she would borrow these good ideas for her own work.

As soon as Mary completed her course at Moody Institute in 1895, she applied for a mission in Africa. To her bitter disappointment, the Board of Missions told her they had no station open to a twenty-year-old girl.

"It was the greatest disappointment of my life," she said later. "Those were cruel days."

Mary traveled home to tell her family and Miss Emma Wilson that she was a failure. But Miss Wilson was not yet back in Mayesville for the fall semester. Local property owners had convinced the school board to shorten the term from four months to two months a year. What did those share-cropping darky children need to do with school, anyway? Two months was plenty long enough for the likes of them to waste on book learning.

Mary decided to open Miss Wilson's school herself, and keep it running until Miss Wilson arrived.

She scrubbed the schoolroom floor. She dusted off the books. She walked around to all her Mayesville neighbors, telling them the school would be open if they wished to send their children.

On November first Mary rang the old school bell and watched the shabbily dressed children file in. Some twenty young faces turned up toward her. As the days passed, she and these youngsters would come to know one another well. Mary would discover the joy of teaching those who were hungry to learn.

She smoothed her blue skirt and stood a little taller. "Good morning, children," she said. "My name is Miss McLeod."

2

It didn't take Miss McLeod long to learn something herself: She was a born teacher. All the energy Mary had built up for working as a missionary in Africa could be used right here at home. "The drums of Africa still beat in my heart," she said many years later. "They will never let me rest while there is a single Negro boy or girl without a chance to prove his worth."

Miss Wilson came back to her school in Mayesville around Christmas time, and Mary McLeod got herself a job teaching at a private school for Negroes— the Haines Institute in Augusta, Georgia. As Mary taught mathematics and raised her rich contralto voice with the Haines school choir, her head was full of dreams about helping the thousands of darkskinned children who never had a chance.

In those days, a quarter of a century after the Civil War, most Negro children in the deep south were still in deep darkness. Sixty percent of them could neither read nor write. By law, each state was supposed to provide public schools for its people. But an average of ninety-three cents out of every dollar spent on education in the South went to schools for white children. This left seven cents for Negro grade schools. Not a single public high school accepted a single Negro pupil.

There were private schools for Negro children, most of them supported by religious groups. The Haines Institute, where Mary taught, happened to be a fine private school, with a library and a staff of well-prepared teachers. But the great majority of the mission schools were makeshift one-room places located in former barns or log-cabin churches. Most of these schools did not go above the seventh grade.

After several years of teaching at Haines, Mary moved on to the Kendall Institute in Sumter, North Carolina, where she continued to dream about opening a school of her own. Here she met and married a fellow teacher, Alburtus Bethune. The young couple moved to Savannah, Georgia, where their son Albert was born, and then on to Palatka, Florida.

Except for a short time while Albert was tiny, Mrs. Bethune continued to teach. While she taught, she took steps to make her dream come true. Later she wrote, "When I accumulated a bit of money

I was off on an exploring trip, seeking a location where a new school would do the greatest good for the greatest number."

On one of her exploring trips Mrs. Bethune found a community in desperate need of a school: Daytona, Florida. Daytona was a booming vacation city. Wealthy white people were beginning to flock there in wintertime, to enjoy the warm climate and the fine beach. Railroad tracks were going down, and big resort hotels were going up. Hundreds of Negro families were pouring into Daytona, lured by the work on railroad gangs and building crews, in hotel kitchens and wealthy homes. Without training, the children of these people faced lives of the same ugly sort their parents were trapped in.

Alburtus was reluctant to move again, but Mary always did what she set out to do. She tidied up the two-room cottage and fixed some food. She packed clothes for herself and little Albert. And she got her husband to promise that he might come on to Daytona later—if Mary wasn't forced to return home first. Then with all the cash they had on hand—$1.50—she set forth down the road with little Albert to beg a ride to Daytona, seventy miles away.

When they got to Daytona Mrs. Bethune and Albert stayed with a hospitable family while Mary got her bearings. The neighbors she talked to were not encouraging.

"How can you begin to do any good with just one puny school!" they said. "Negroes who forget their place just get into trouble around here."

Mrs. Bethune listened but did not hear. She roamed the Negro section of town, looking for a place for her school. Down at the edge of the city, close to the ocean, next to a dumping ground, she found a ramshackle cottage. The porch floor sagged and the paint was gone, but the building had four rooms downstairs and three above, and it was for rent.

The white owner thought Mrs. Bethune's reason for wanting the cottage was ridiculous. "We don't need another nigger school here in Volusia County," he said, meaning to be kind. "There's already one down at the Colored Baptist Church—goes clear up to third grade. That's as far as any darky has the sense to learn."

But he agreed to rent the cottage for eleven dollars a month. When Mrs. Bethune confessed she did not have eleven dollars, he accepted fifty cents as a down payment. After all, he figured, the cottage was falling to pieces with nobody living in it.

Next Mrs. Bethune, with little Albert tagging along at her side, toured the construction camps looking for pupils. Not too many of these workers were interested in an education for their children, or had the money to spare. But she found five girls, aged eight to twelve, whose parents were willing to pay a tuition fee of fifty cents a week.

Mrs. Bethune spent hours scouring every dump heap in town. She was looking for pieces of lumber, broken furniture, old lamps and washtubs, cracked mirrors—anything that could be used. She knocked at the back doors of white people's houses, begging for anything from pennies to nails. Some people gave her money. Others let her cart off their chipped dishes, torn linens, extra pots.

Everything was cleaned and mended, and Mrs. Bethune repaired and furnished the cottage with these bits and pieces. Later she described it: "I lay awake nights, contriving how to turn peach baskets into chairs. People laughed at my makeshifts. The members of my own race called after me: 'There goes the beggar!' And many white folks gave me their leftovers just to get rid of me."

Mrs. Bethune burned logs and carefully collected charred splinters to use instead of pencils. She never passed a hen house without stopping to collect feathers to use as pens. She made ink by squeezing elderberries. She turned a packing case into a desk for herself, and decorated it with a bit of printed cretonne. "This was all part of the training," she said, "to salvage, to reconstruct, to make bricks without straw."

But even the remarkable Mrs. Bethune could not manage entirely without cash. She found a way to earn money by using a friend's kitchen to bake toothsome batches of sweet-potato pies. She took the fragrant hot pies down to the construction camps and sold them by the slice.

With the girls' help, Mrs. Bethune gathered moss from live-oak trees and stuffed it into sacks to make

mattresses. She carefully dusted off her library and laid it out on the packing-case desk. Six books! There was a Bible, a blue-backed speller, a geography book and one on algebra, a songbook and one volume of poetry by John Greenleaf Whittier. This last was a lovely leather-bound edition. Alburtus had given it to her, back in their courting days.

In one month the cottage was ready. The Daytona Educational and Industrial Training School for Negro Girls opened its doors on October 3, 1904. There was a simple ceremony first, before a handful of well-wishers.

"This is a new kind of school," said Mrs. Bethune to her friends. "I am going to teach my girls crafts and home-making. I am going to teach them to earn a living. They will be trained in head, hand, and heart: their heads to think, their hands to work, and their hearts to have faith."

Standing outdoors in front of the cottage, Mrs. Bethune led her five pupils and Albert in the singing

of the 23rd Psalm: "The Lord is my Shepherd, I shall not want . . ."

She offered a brief prayer: "We thank Thee, Lord, for this school building. Let these girls enter to learn; let them depart to serve."

Then the principal and her charges marched inside and Mrs. Bethune settled down to hoe the long, hard row that lay ahead. She had an empty purse, to be sure, but her fund of zeal was so immense no bank could hope to hold it.

Life at school fell into a regular channel: half a day for lessons, half a day for work to keep body and soul together. Mrs. Bethune continued to bake her sweet-potato pies. She rode a patched-up bicycle across the peninsula into the handsome part of town and sold her pies to guests at the resort hotels.

Mrs. Bethune made friends with some of the resort people. A few of the gentlemen developed the habit of taking a morning stroll down to the hotel entrance. There they would buy a piece of sweet-potato pie and chat with the deep-voiced woman who sold it. She was stout and broad-featured, but there was a shining quality about her that made beauty unimportant. Some white people began to feel it was entirely respectable to be interested in a school for Negro children—especially if the children learned humbleness and service along with a little simple arithmetic and reading.

Mrs. Bethune did not quarrel with their idea. She

knew her girls had to learn to cook and serve, because jobs such as these were the only ones open to them when they grew up. But in her heart she was still dreaming—dreaming of the day when people of her race could take their full places in the community. Someday her students would go forth to become business leaders and scientists, statesmen and nurses and doctors, lawyers and teachers, contributing to the community according to their abilities.

A dignified gentleman named James N. Gamble became one of Mrs. Bethune's steadiest pie customers. She often described her school to him. Its main building was called Faith Hall, she said. It contained a library and a chapel as well as schoolrooms and living quarters. "I would like you to become one of the school's trustees," she told him.

One morning just before the end of the winter tourist season, a stately limousine drew up before the school and a chauffeur helped Mr. Gamble step out. He looked around. Faith Hall? A beautifully planted campus? Uniformed students?

What Mr. Gamble saw was an outside shed rigged up near the cottage to serve as a kitchen. Several of the girls were peeling hot sweet potatoes, dropping them into a steaming pot for Mrs. Bethune to mash. One girl was reading aloud from the geography book. Little Albert played quietly under a nearby tree.

Mrs. Bethune took off her apron and walked to greet Mr. Gamble. They looked one another in the eye. "And where is the school of which you want me to be trustee?" Mr. Gamble said sternly.

"In my mind and in my soul," answered Mary Bethune. "I am asking you to be trustee of a glorious dream, trustee of the hope I have in my heart for my people."

There was another moment of silence. Then Mr. Gamble reached for his checkbook. "I'll be back next winter," he said, writing out a check, "and I hope to be present on that day when your Faith Hall is dedicated."

Mrs. Bethune's school grew quickly, and so did her problems. She added grades as she added pupils. In less than two years there were two hundred and fifty pupils and four teachers. Many of the pupils lived at the school. So did the teachers, who were each paid $3.50 a week besides room and board. Many a dinner was nothing more than black-eyed peas and hominy grits. Mrs. Bethune rented another shack next door to her first cottage, but she was in desperate need of space, supplies, and money.

When Mrs. Bethune's shoes wore through, she cut new soles out of cardboard. She trained her girls to sing Negro folk songs and spirituals and sent them out into the community to sing for money. Soon it was fashionable to invite them to sing in white churches, hotels, and private drawing rooms for the entertainment of guests.

Mrs. Bethune redoubled her appeals: "I learned . . . that one of my most important jobs was to be a good beggar! I rang doorbells and tackled cold prospects without a lead. I wrote articles for whoever would print them, distributed leaflets, rode interminable miles of dusty roads on my old bicycle, invaded churches, clubs, lodges, chambers of commerce. If a prospect refused to make a contribution, I would say, 'Thank you for your time.' No matter how deep my hurt, I always smiled. I refused to be discouraged, for neither God nor man can use a discouraged person."

By this time the school offered night classes for adults three times a week. These men and women had daytime jobs as janitors, garbage collectors, cleaning women, and the like. They were often able to bring Mrs. Bethune such treasures as old newspapers, discarded clothes, a sack of corn meal, an abandoned ice-cream freezer. Sometimes they even had money for the school, slipped to them by "the lady of the house," who admired Mrs. Bethune's courage but didn't dare support a Negro school openly.

"I was supposed to keep the balance of the funds for my own pocket, but there never was any balance— only a yawning hole," said Mrs. Bethune. "At last I saw that our only solution was to stop renting space and to buy and build our own college."

Where? Again Mrs. Bethune combed the possible neighborhood from one end to another. Finally she settled on a swampy dumping ground on Oak Street, known as Hell's Hole. She located the owner.

"What, you want to buy that dump heap?" he asked.

"I don't see a dump heap!" said Mrs. Bethune. "I see thousands of boys and girls, walking through open doors."

They settled on a price of two hundred dollars, with a down payment of five dollars. "He never knew it, but I didn't have five dollars," Mrs. Bethune wrote later. "I promised to be back in a few days with the initial payment. I raised this sum selling ice-cream and sweet-potato pies to the workmen on construction jobs, and I took the owner his money in small change wrapped in my handkerchief."

Some of the workmen were also friends of Mrs. Bethune's school. In their free time they helped her drain the swamp. They burned all the trash that would burn, and buried the rest. Mrs. Bethune described the way she "hung on to contractors' coat-tails, begging for loads of sand and second-hand bricks." She went around to carpenters, mechanics, and plasterers, inviting them to parties at the school. They came, ate her delicious desserts, joined in some singing, and then "first thing you know, those men got in the mood to do a bit of work for me, on the spot, free of charge. After a while, those coffee parties of mine became sort of famous."

And so, slowly but surely, a four-story wooden building with an open front porch took shape. As soon as there was a roof over part of it, Mrs. Bethune moved students in. Now and then, whenever she ran out of funds, work stopped until she raised more money. But in two years the building had been "prayed up, sung up, and talked up," and in 1907 Faith Hall officially opened. "Enter to Learn," said a motto over the front entrance. Inside the same door were the words, "Depart to Serve."

With the help of her pupils and one hired man, Mrs. Bethune filled in the rest of the swamp by the school and planted a garden. Soon they had sugar cane and sweet potatoes, snap beans and strawberries. The finest specimens were sold from a wooden roadside stand. People drove miles to this out-of-the-way place to buy succulent fruits and vegetables.

While people bought produce, Mrs. Bethune exercised her talent for persuasion. One tourist from Ridgewood, New Jersey, contributed seventy-five dollars. Mrs. Bethune promptly bought a cow and courteously named it "Ridgewood." A Longmeadow, Massachusetts, lady contributed another cow and it was suitably called "Longmeadow." Soon the school also owned a mule and three pigs.

The job of running the school grew until it became impossible for one person to manage everything. At about this time, Mrs. Bethune named one of the four teachers, Mrs. Frances Keyser, as acting principal. This gave Mrs. Bethune time to concentrate on the vital job of finding money.

But Mrs. Bethune continued to keep her own bright eyes on what was going on in the classrooms. The girls could expect her to pop in and out, asking questions that were embarrassing if they hadn't done their homework. And woe to the pupil who walked past a scrap of paper. Mrs. Bethune would materialize out of nowhere and say, "How can you pass litter without picking it up! Don't be lazy!"

Mrs. Bethune inspected rooms regularly, to see that beds were made, closets neat, and girls themselves well washed and tidy. She had a habit of tacking up her handwritten mottoes on schoolroom walls. "Blessed is he that readeth," they would say, or "Speak softly, save your voice for songs of praise."

Everybody cleaned, sewed, learned to bake bread, prepare and serve delicious food, and sing. The sing-

ing was so successful in raising money for the school
that Mrs. Bethune often took her neatly uniformed
group on singing tours in the North.

Now the school's curriculum ran through high
school. It was turning out graduates trained for
homemaking, teaching, and nursing. But Faith Hall
was full to overflowing almost as soon as it was

built. Another building was urgently needed.

As usual, Mrs. Bethune found the money. A large
brick building went up. It was called White Hall
because most of the money for it was given by a
man named Thomas H. White.

The opening ceremony, in 1916, was strikingly
different from the straggly little dedication of the
cottage back in 1904. This time there was a dignified

procession of teachers in caps and gowns marching into the chapel to the music of the school band. Every one of the six hundred seats in the auditorium was filled. The audience listened to speeches by the vice-president of the United States, and the governor of Florida. Mrs. Bethune accepted the keys to the new building. Her hand trembled a little as she passed them along to James N. Gamble, president of her board of trustees.

While the school was becoming firmly established, Mrs. Bethune's energies overflowed into the community in ever-widening circles as ripples flow out from a pebble thrown into a pond. Her first interest was her school, but she had room left over to tackle other problems—the turpentine camps, for instance. These were filthy settlements in the pine woods. Men who formerly worked to complete the railroads now gathered sticky pitch to be distilled into turpentine. These men and their families lived on miserable incomes in almost indescribable disease and ugliness.

Other people shuddered and turned their backs, but not Mrs. Bethune. Within five years she had five mission schools in operation, staffed by students from her own school. Camp children learned to read and write, and their mothers learned to cook and sew. Their fathers began to earn better wages and spend less of it on drink.

During the same period, Mrs. Bethune found time

to sponsor various other projects. One day, at school, she was called to the bedside of a student weeping with pain. The young Negro doctor who came hurrying over said, "She has acute appendicitis. She needs an immediate operation."

There was no hospital in Daytona Beach where Negro doctors could operate or Negro patients could recover. Mrs. Bethune hurried to a white surgeon and begged him to help her sick youngster. Moved by her desperate pleading, the doctor agreed.

But when Mrs. Bethune visited the girl in the hospital the next day, she found Clara lying on a drafty back-porch cot. It was hard for her to recover from the operation when she felt sickened by smells from the adjoining kitchen.

This was a call to action for Mrs. Bethune. She located another cottage to buy. She figured up costs for an operating table, instruments, two beds, sheets, blankets—five thousand dollars would do it. As usual, her pleading letters went out across the country, written to everybody she could think of. In a month she had the money, and in two months the tiny two-bed hospital stood ready to serve. She named it McLeod Hospital, to honor her now-dead father. As time went on, the hospital grew. It had to. It was another twenty years before the city of Daytona Beach built a public hospital for its Negro citizens.

The day McLeod Hospital opened, Mary Bethune allowed herself one very special luxury: She sent a railroad ticket to her mother. Old Patsy McLeod had never been on a train, had never set eyes on her grandson Albert, had never seen Faith Hall, with its trim grounds and abundant gardens. Now she came to enjoy these pleasures. She saw her daughter Mary, loved and respected, guiding the lives of hundreds of energetic, hopeful young people.

From time to time, there were other visitors from Mrs. Bethune's past. Miss Mary Crissman, the Quaker seamstress, came from Denver to see the Negro girl "you are sure will make good."

And Alburtus came to Daytona Beach. Through the years he and his wife had kept in touch with friendly letters. For a time he thought he might settle in Daytona. He looked around for work but could find only a job as a hackie, driving a horse and buggy. When young Albert left Daytona to attend high school at Haines Institute, Alburtus took a teaching job in a boys' school in Georgia. He died there in 1919.

Running a school, creating a hospital, and establishing mission schools at the turpentine camps did not take all of Mrs. Bethune's boundless energy. She was also active in many national clubs. The groups she joined were those working for the same principles she held dear—improving the lot of her people.

Mrs. Bethune knew that Negroes must vote if they were ever to take their full places in the community. But Southern states had many legal tricks for keeping Negroes from the polls. There was the poll tax, which most Negroes could not afford. Or a stiff literacy test, much too difficult for a poorly educated people. Or voting practices which were meant to be confusing, such as requiring a different ballot box for every office voted upon.

Some Southerners did not depend on legal tricks alone. Of those who believed in white supremacy, none worked more fiercely to keep the Negro "in his place" than the members of a terror organization called the Ku Klux Klan. White men, hooded in sheets to resemble ghosts, marched through the countryside at night. They terrified the superstitious, ignorant Negroes. They often turned terror to horror by means of fires, beatings, or lynchings.

But Mrs. Bethune moved stanchly forward in her fight to get her people to the polls. She held night classes in civics. She rode her old bicycle up and down the streets of the colored quarter, urging citizens to pay their poll tax. By prodding and lecturing, begging and praying, she managed to get almost a hundred Negro citizens in Volusia County registered to vote. Eleven of them were teachers from her own school, for "the Susan B. Anthony amendment," allowing women to vote, had just been added to the law of the land.

One day, shortly before the 1920 elections, a rumor reached the school: The Klan was going to march that night, as a warning to Mrs. Bethune. They wanted to stop her political activity.

Perhaps the Klan leaders did not know that Mrs.

Bethune was in New York that day, lecturing to raise money for the Red Cross. Mrs. Frances Keyser was in charge of the school. She called the older girls together and told them about the rumor. Then, in order not to frighten the younger children, they finished out the day as though it were any other day.

At last the little ones were safely in bed. Then Mrs. Keyser, the other teachers, and the older girls gathered at the front windows of the school. They huddled together in the dark and waited . . .

Soon a flicker of torches appeared. It came closer and closer. Hooded men on hooded horses appeared out of the darkness and behind them a rabble of masked men on foot. Carrying flaming torches the procession turned in at the school driveway. They marched menacingly past the front entrance and out again into the night. Glory be to God, this visit was "only" a warning.

Mrs. Bethune hurried home. She expected the Klan to march again on election eve, and it did. Mrs. Bethune was ready. She raised every blind in the school. She turned on every light. It was choir practice night, and she instructed the girls to sing as usual. Then Mrs. Bethune, alone, wearing a long white cape, took up a commanding position on the front porch.

A teacher protested, "Don't make a target of yourself. They might kill you!"

"I am going to stand in the light as a symbol of

freedom," said Mrs. Bethune. "It is *they* who are the figures of darkness."

Time passed. The sweet voices of the girls drifted into the November night.

Be not dismayed whate'er betide
God will take care of us!

Again, that flicker of torches. A bloodcurdling blast from some weird horn. Blazing emblems. A procession of about eighty shrouded men. The parade came up the driveway and halted. A cluster of six men shuffled up to Mrs. Bethune. One man carried a large can of kerosene.

From behind the mask came his muffled voice, "We're warning you! Stop filling nigger heads with ideas about voting. Do you want us to burn every building here right down to the ground?"

Behind Mrs. Bethune the choir sang:

My soul is anchored in the Lord,
No man can harm me.

"Burn my buildings if you must, you cowards!" replied Mrs. Bethune in a voice that was husky with anger. "I'll build them right back again! The forces of evil shall not prevail!"

The men wavered and fell back. After a few moments of indecision they melted away, leaving their kerosene can standing on the lawn. The handy-

man came out and picked it up.

"Good," said Mrs. Bethune. The school could always use an extra can of kerosene.

When election day dawned, a different sort of procession marched in Daytona. "The next morning," reported Mrs. Bethune, "I was standing at the polling place at eight o'clock to vote with a line of Negroes behind me. They kept us waiting all day, but *we voted!*"

In 1923 Mrs. Bethune's school merged with a men's college, Cookman Institute, operated by the Methodist Episcopal Church. Mrs. Bethune remained as president of the new Bethune-Cookman Junior College with its 600 students, 32 teachers, and 14 buildings on 32 acres of campus.

She was nearing fifty, an age when most people begin to slow up. But Mrs. Bethune was never like most people. She lived to be almost eighty, and her last thirty years were busier, if possible, than her first half a century.

Mrs. Bethune often worked until midnight, and then called her secretary again at four o'clock in the morning. Once, when Mrs. Bethune was over seventy, a sculptor named Ruth Brall was trying to sketch her. Mrs. Brall complained that she lost ten pounds whisking around after her subject. Finally she had to say, "Please, Mrs. Bethune. I can work all day, or all night; I can't do both."

Mrs. Bethune was in great demand as a speaker.

One year she talked at more than five hundred meetings in forty states. She was an imposing figure with her white hair, her majestic bulk, and the heavy cane she always carried "for swank." But it was her message that people came to hear, her eloquence as she asked the country to "let my people go."

"In order to know which way a tree is growing," she said, "we must watch its upper branches: those of the race who have accomplished something and are leaders. The race should be judged by that group rather than the masses who have not had their chance to develop."

Wherever she went, Mrs. Bethune told her own people, "Walk proudly in the light! Faith ought not to be a puny thing. If we believe, we should believe like giants." Young people adored her, and she became known as "the First Lady" of her race.

She was a close friend of another "First Lady," Mrs. Eleanor Roosevelt. President Franklin Delano Roosevelt often made use of Mrs. Bethune's wisdom and knowledge. He named her Director of Negro Affairs when he established a National Youth Administration to help young people find employment during the severe business depression of the 1930s. He appointed her Special Civilian Assistant when he set up the first United States Women's Army Corps during World War II. She was a frequent visitor to the White House. President Roosevelt said he was always glad to see Mrs. Bethune because she never asked anything for herself.

Mrs. Bethune told her friends, "I never walk through the White House door without wondering how all this happened to a child from the cotton fields."

All her life, wherever she went, Mrs. Bethune insisted on her rights as a human being. Often, traveling around the country, she would run into restaurant owners who would not serve her, elevator men who would not let her ride, train conductors who would rudely say, "Gimme your ticket, Auntie!" Mrs. Bethune would smile and ask, "And which one of my sister's children are you?"

In 1940 she spent some weeks in Baltimore's Johns Hopkins Hospital. Mrs. Bethune suffered badly from asthma, and her doctor hoped an operation on her nose would relieve her breathing. Negroes did not usually get private rooms at the hospital, but because Mrs. Bethune was well known, a special room was set up for her.

At that time neither doctors nor nurses could work at Johns Hopkins Hospital if they were Negro. When Mrs. Bethune arrived at the hospital a young white woman came into her room and said, "Mary, I'm going to be your nurse."

"You are not my friend or relative that you can call me by my first name," said Mrs. Bethune.

The nurse apologized. She told the story all over the hospital, but apparently it did not reach the ears of the surgeon who later operated on Mrs. Bethune.

[114]

"Turn your head, Mary," he instructed as she lay on the operating table.

Drowsy with drugs and her nose full of instruments, Mrs. Bethune could not talk back. But next morning when the surgeon came around to see how she was, she explained how she felt.

"Forgive me, Mrs. Bethune," said the doctor. "I spoke out of habit, but meant no discourtesy."

That afternoon a huge basket of flowers arrived in Mrs. Bethune's room. A nurse said it was the first time in all the surgeon's years that he had sent flowers to a patient.

When the first meeting of the United Nations was held in San Francisco in April of 1945, Mrs. Bethune was present. She was deeply interested in this newly forming organization with its determination "to reaffirm faith in fundamental human rights, in the dignity and worth of the human person, in the equal rights of men and women and of nations large and small."

In all her life's work Mrs. Bethune had been part of the progress of the Negro race. She was delighted to be able to say now, "I have come to the point where I can embrace all humanity—not just the people of my race or another race. I just love people."

The recently widowed Mrs. Eleanor Roosevelt was at the United Nations meeting, too. She gave Mrs. Bethune one of President Roosevelt's canes, as a memento of their long, warm friendship.

Mrs. Bethune used this cane until the day she died. It was in her hand one hot morning in 1950 when she walked slowly down the dirt road in Mayesville, South Carolina. She had returned to her old home town for one last look around.

Many things were changed. There was not a trace of the cabin her father had built. All the faces were different in the sharecroppers' shanties. But down at the end of the road, next to the railroad tracks, Miss Wilson's old school was still standing. It was pitifully shabby. It was still—sixty years later—the only school open to the Negro children of Mayesville.

But, by God's gift, the aged, ailing Mrs. Bethune lived long enough to know that Miss Wilson's old school would not need to stand much longer. On May 17, 1954, the Supreme Court of the United States ruled that Negro children and white children across the nation must be allowed to go to school together.

And so, when Mary McLeod Bethune's heart stopped beating on May 18, 1955, she died in the peace of a dream that would soon be real: "There is no such thing as Negro education—only education. I want my people to prepare themselves bravely for life, not because they are Negroes, but because they are men."

AMELIA EARHART

"Flying Is Fun"

1

Late in 1961 a professor of anthropology at the University of California received a package from the island of Saipan in the Pacific. In the package were seven pounds of human teeth and bones. The professor was being asked for his expert opinion on a very important question: Are these the remains of the missing flier, Amelia Earhart?

Amelia Earhart had been one of those rare creatures in the early days of airplanes—a woman pilot. She was tall, skinny, and charming. She had gray eyes, tousled hair, a breezy manner, and a wide smile. Between 1928 and 1937 she captured the imagination of millions of armchair adventurers.

In those days airplanes were still so rare that people rushed outdoors to crane their necks when one swooped by overhead. Yet there was A.E. (as she called herself) cruising about the sky in a frail aircraft, making and breaking world records. Rapid, nonstop, luxurious flights in multi-passenger jets were twenty-five years away. In the world of air travel, these were the pioneer times.

By 1937 Amelia Earhart's name was a household word. When she and her navigator, Fred Noonan, disappeared one July day during a flight around the world, many people refused to believe that A.E.'s flashing grace was gone forever. They hoped she had brought her plane down safely. A legend grew that she had been on a secret mission for the government and that her plane was shot down by the Japanese. She had been captured, said the story. Either she and Noonan had been shot as spies, or they were living as prisoners somewhere on a Pacific island.

Late in the 1950's a San Francisco newsman began to look for answers to the Earhart mystery. Many residents of Saipan, he found, insisted that a white woman had once lived there. They could point to her grave. Soldiers stationed on the island during World War II reported seeing snapshots of her. One soldier claimed he had seen a photograph of Miss Earhart standing near Japanese aircraft on an airfield.

So the newsman traveled to Saipan, took the bones from their island grave, and brought them back to the University of California. On December 5, 1961, The New York *Times* reported the results of the professor's careful analysis: AMELIA EARHART CLUE FAILS; SAIPAN BONES ARE NOT HERS.

This is the life story of Amelia Mary Earhart . . .

She was born in Atchison, Kansas, on July 24, 1898. Her father was a lawyer for the Rock Island Railway and his job kept the family on the move. Sometimes A.E. and her sister Muriel stayed in Atchison with their grandmother Otis. Other times they lived with their parents, attending one school after another as they shifted around the country with their father's jobs. Amelia went to six high schools in four years. When she graduated from Hyde Park High School in Chicago a classmate wrote under her yearbook picture, "The girl in brown who walks alone."

Amelia continued to walk alone as she cast about for something to satisfy her. For a while she went to a private school near Philadelphia. But World War I was raging in Europe, and she wanted to help. She went to Toronto, Canada, and took a job as a nurses' aid. From her hospital experience she developed an interest in medicine. She enrolled at Columbia University in New York City, intending to become a doctor. Many years later A.E. wrote, "I've had twenty-eight different jobs in my life, and I hope I'll have two hundred and twenty-eight more. Experiment! Meet new people! That's better than any college education. You will find the unexpected everywhere as you go through life."

After a winter at Columbia University, Amelia traveled to California to spend the summer holiday with her family. It was here she stumbled on her own "unexpected" in life.

It happened on a Sunday afternoon when Amelia and her father watched daring young sportsmen flying their planes at an air meet in Long Beach, California. Moved by a sudden impulse, Amelia begged her father to talk to one of the barnstorming pilots. "Ask him how long it takes to learn how to fly," she urged, "and find out how much it costs."

Mr. Earhart was an agreeable man, so he found out. "It takes anywhere from five to ten hours to learn how to fly," he reported. "And it costs about a thousand dollars, so of course it is absolutely out of the question for you."

They went home, but Amelia could not forget airplanes. Like a nail to a magnet, she returned to the tiny flying field—a stretch of space surrounded by oil wells. She paid for a ride, and Frank Hawks took her aloft for a spin.

"As soon as we left the ground," Amelia said later, "I knew I had to fly by myself. Miles away I saw the ocean . . . the Hollywood hills smiled at me over the edge of the cockpit . . . We were friends, the ocean, the hills, and I."

A.E. left her heart in the sky, but she still had to earn a living on the ground. She took a job, first with a telephone company and later in a photographic studio, and spent her salary on flying lessons.

On a shopping trip one day she saw a gorgeous patent-leather flying coat—just the thing for a professional pilot to wear. She paid twenty dollars for it and went dancing home, but when she unwrapped the coat and looked at it again it was disappointingly shiny and new. It lacked the old-time beat-up look a veteran flier's coat would have. It needed wrinkles! A.E. found an effective treatment: for three nights she wore the coat to bed over her nightgown.

During the next several years A.E. flew wherever and whenever she could. She didn't imagine she could earn a living by flying, however, so she kept looking for work that would be satisfying. Her sister Muriel was a teacher, so A.E. thought she would try her hand at teaching. She attended a summer school at Harvard University, and later secured a sixty-dollar-a-month job teaching at the Denison Settlement House in Boston.

One busy morning while she was teaching English to a noisy class of Italian, Chinese, and Syrian children, Miss Earhart was called to the office to answer the telephone. "Miss Earhart," a voice said, "are you still interested in flying?" What did the caller have in mind? A.E. visited his office and found he was asking her to be a passenger in a flight across the Atlantic.

In 1928 flying across the Atlantic Ocean was not an ordinary experience for a man, and no woman had ever done it. Now two men, pilot Wilmer ("Bill")

Stultz and mechanic Lou ("Slim") Gordon, were about to cross in an airplane, the *Friendship*. The wealthy woman sponsoring their flight wanted a woman aboard too. The tri-motored *Friendship* was a trim airship, with a spread of seventy-two feet. Her body was red-orange, her wings were gold, and she was equipped with pontoons—floats which make it possible for a plane to land on water. A.E. was eager to go along for the ride, even though she would be only a passenger.

After long weeks of preparation, the *Friendship* took off from Boston harbor one Sunday morning and flew up to the tiny fishing village of Trepassey, Newfoundland. This northern island juts into the ocean and makes the shortest possible direct route from the continent of America to the shores of England. The *Friendship's* journey was to end at Southampton on the English Channel.

Planes of 1928 rode the skies at the mercy of winds and weather. They could not store enough extra gasoline to fight against high winds for any great distance. They were not equipped with heated and pressurized cabins that would allow pilots to take their craft into cold, thin air high above any storm. So Stultz and Gordon, together with their lone lady passenger, sat at Trepassey trapped by the weather reports. It was foggy and damp. They ate canned rabbit and boiled mutton and tried to amuse themselves with fishing and hiking, while day after day the radio delivered its miserable weather tidings.

Two long weeks dragged by. There had been so many false starts that almost nobody was at hand to see them off when, early in the morning of June 17, the *Friendship* taxied down the harbor and lifted herself heavily into the air.

Nor was there a reception committee when they landed, exactly twenty hours and forty minutes later. They were short of gas and somewhat off course, so instead of coming down at Southampton they touched water in the harbor of Burry Port, South Wales.

It was a dull, rainy day. Except for some workmen down by the railroad, few citizens were stirring on the streets of Burry Port. None of them paid any attention to the *Friendship*. Stultz and Gordon crawled out on a pontoon and shouted. No response. A.E. leaned out the window and madly waved a white towel. One of the workmen took off his coat and playfully waved back.

At last, an hour or so later, some policemen rowed out to the bobbing airplane. "Do you be wanting something?" asked the leader.

"We've come from America," said the crew of the *Friendship*.

"Have ye now? Well, we wish ye welcome, I'm sure . . ."

As it turned out, the *Friendship* flight meant more than friendship for A.E.—it was the beginning of romance. George Palmer Putnam was one of the

arrangers of the flight, and he continued to help and encourage A.E., as he was soon calling her, in other adventures. "Encourage" was not always what he did, however. There was the time, for instance, when he wrote her a letter and said, "Your hats! They are a public menace. You should do something about them when you must wear them at all!"

Whether or not his advice had anything to do with it, A.E. never wore a hat if she could get by without one. As time went on her short, wind-swept hair became familiar to millions. Her favorite clothes were tailored slacks, worn with a silk shirt and a bright scarf.

During the next few years George Palmer Putnam kept asking A.E. to marry him and A.E. kept refusing. She could not picture herself settling down in a kitchen. Her kitchen was the cockpit of a plane. For Amelia Earhart flying was knitted tightly into life itself.

But Putnam understood her need to be free, and promised he would never keep her from flying.

In February of 1931, Amelia Earhart finally became Mrs. George Palmer Putnam in a quiet wedding at the home of her husband's mother. Just before the ceremony she solemnly handed her bridegroom a note. It read, ". . . Please let us not interfere with the other's work or play, nor let the world see our private joys or disagreements. . . . I may have to keep some place where I can go to be myself now and then, for I cannot guarantee to endure at all times the confinements of even an attractive cage. . . . I will try to do my best in every way . . ."

After their marriage, as before it, Putnam continued to help A.E. in her projects. She did not like to talk about her private life, but when people asked her she would say, "Ours is a reasonable and contented partnership, my husband with his solo jobs and I with mine; but the system of dual control works satisfactorily and our work and our play is a great deal together."

From the day Amelia Earhart crossed the Atlantic as a passenger in the *Friendship,* she longed to do it again, alone. By 1932 she had flown more than a thousand hours. She now owned a bright-red second-hand Lockheed Vega in which she planned to install a brand-new Wasp motor, so it would be capable of long-distance flying.

Carefully, quietly, she prepared the plane and herself. When a pilot has to fly "blind," the instruments are his eyes. Among the instruments in her little plane was an altimeter to record how high over the ocean she flew. There was a barograph to tell whether the plane was climbing or dropping, and a tachometer to tell how fast she was going. "Such instruments are vital," explained A.E., "because when it is dark or foggy it is almost impossible to know whether one is flying upside down or right side up, whether one is climbing safely or headed for swift destruction."

A.E. filled the Lockheed with many gallons of gas

and oil for the motor, but took only a thermos bottle of soup and a can of tomato juice for herself. She carried no baggage beyond the clothes on her back: jodhpurs, a silk shirt, a windbreaker, and a leather flying suit. Friends urged her to pack some spare clothes and extra food for herself. She told them that extra clothes and food would mean extra weight and extra worry. "A pilot whose plane falls into the Atlantic is not consoled by caviar sandwiches!"

So it came about that on the evening of May 20, 1932, A.E. again took off from Newfoundland into the east where the sun would rise. Through the quiet night she flew, alone with the stars. They dotted the sky like daisies in a meadow. It seemed as though A.E. could pick a bouquet of stars simply by reaching out through her cockpit window. Far below, contrasting with the starlight, lay the restless black ocean. A.E. was a tiny grain of life, adrift in the endless universe.

Clouds came and sat over the face of the moon. A storm blew up. Lightning crackled and thunder roared. The little plane shivered and rocked. It was pitch dark beyond her windshield. The pilot could see nothing but her dimly lit control panel with its array of life-saving instruments.

And then the altimeter failed. Its dials swung insanely, recording nothing. A.E. saw an opening in the clouds and tilted her plane upward. Perhaps she could fly high enough to get above the storm. For half an hour she nosed her plane up and up. A.E.

saw dangerous slush on her windows and ice on the wings of her plane. Cold air froze the tachometer and suddenly her machine went into a deadly spin. The barograph recorded an almost straight drop of 3,000 feet.

"How long we spun I do not know," A.E. wrote later. "I do know that I tried my best to do exactly what one should do with a spinning plane, and regained flying control as the warmth of the lower altitude melted the ice. As we righted and held level again, through the blackness below I could see the whitecaps too close for comfort."

She went through five hours of hammering storm before she could fly peacefully once more, alone with her thoughts. But fate was not through playing with her that night. A.E. noticed a little tail of flame flickering from the pipe which carried exhaust gas from the motor. Such a fire would slowly eat its way through the metal pipe and then—— "Would I rather die by drowning or burning?" thought A.E.

"Neither, really," she told herself. But there was nothing she could do about it. It was no use turning back, for she couldn't land at Harbor Grace in the dark. She might just as well keep going.

Keep going she did, and soon it was earliest dawn. The leak of flame did not look so ominous in the pearly light, and A.E. saw little puffs of cloud hanging right over the water "like fluffy mashed potatoes." The sun came up, so bright that A.E. had to put on dark glasses.

"Early morning is the best time," she wrote later. "Even the air seems to have dew on it. It's sweet and heavy and smooth, and a plane can bite into it."

But on this particular morning of May 21 what A.E. wanted was not to fly, but to land. She had switched to her reserve gasoline tanks and discovered a leaky gauge. She must come down, and not be too fussy about where she did it. Her plane was over the tip of Ireland now. Below were bright green fields dotted with grazing cows. A meadow could serve as airfield. Avoiding the cows, she selected an open spot and settled down into farmer Gallagher's pasture. An astonished man appeared. A.E. stuck her head up through the hatch and for the second time said, "I'm from America."

This flight was the real beginning of public life for A.E. In Europe and America she attended receptions and banquets, accepted honors and medals. Sackfuls of fan letters came to her, and many of them were from children. One Kentucky youngster wrote, "Please teach me to fly . . . I will repay you if it takes the rest of my life . . . I haven't got much because my father loads coal in a mine." And from Michigan: "I am 15 years old, 105 pounds, quiet and want to see the world. I have no money, but will work my head of [off]."

In the next five years A.E. was a busy woman. She gave lectures, wrote articles, designed dresses. She also earned more "firsts." She became the first woman to fly an autogiro—an aircraft something like a helicopter—and the first to navigate one across the United States. She was the first woman to receive the Distinguished Flying Cross, presented by the Congress of the United States. In January, 1935, she flew alone across the Pacific from Hawaii to California. In May of that year she flew nonstop from Mexico City to Newark, New Jersey—2,125 miles in 18 hours and 18 minutes.

She did these things, as one reporter wrote, "Not for a record . . . Not for the clamor of the crowd . . . Not for money, not for science, not for 'posterity,' not for anything but the fact that she is that kind of girl, and that kind of flier, and likes that kind of fidelity to personal aspiration."

She was smothered with praise, but A.E. kept her level head. In a file folder labeled "Bunk" she stored all the extravagant letters, poems, songs, and such telegrams as one from a mayor whose city she was about to visit: "Welcome, thrice welcome, grand Lady of the Air, crowned glory of earth's womanhood!"

As long as there are people in the world there will be differences of opinion. This was true about everything Amelia Earhart did. Each time she made a spectacular flight she was showered with criticism as well as praise. She was rash, some held. She was hot-headed. She was a publicity hound. Her flights were nothing more than stunts in a speed-mad age. Flying is a careful science. There is no room in it for useless courage.

A.E. answered her critics this way: "To want in one's heart to do a thing for its own sake . . . isn't, I think, a reason to be apologized for by man or woman. It is the most honest motive for the majority of mankind's achievements."

In 1935 she was invited to join the faculty of Purdue University in Indiana as an adviser in flying. In announcing her appointment Purdue's president, Edward C. Elliott, said: "Miss Earhart represents better than any other young woman of this generation the spirit and the courageous skill of what may be called the new pioneering."

At the university she talked to girl students about their future plans. ". . . if you want to try a certain job, try it," she told them. "Then if you find something . . . that looks better, make a change. And if you should find that you are the first *woman* to feel an urge in that direction—what does it matter? . . . Act on it just the same. It may turn out to be fun. And to me fun is an absolutely necessary part of work."

A.E. was delighted when the Purdue Research Foundation bought her a two-motor Lockheed Electra to use as a "flying laboratory." It had a normal speed of about 180 miles an hour, and could carry enough gasoline to cruise more than 4,000 miles. The cockpit was a cubbyhole about four-and-a-half feet square, enclosed in glass. The instrument panel was studded with more than a hundred knobs and dials—all the latest flying devices. A.E. found it "simply elegant."

Early in 1937 Miss Earhart called a press conference. Reporters and camera men crowded into the New York hotel room. Tall and slim, A.E. stood before them, wearing a blue wool dress and gay scarf. Her hand rested lightly on a globe of the world.

"Well, I'm going to try to fly around the globe as near to the equator as I can make it . . ." she said. Her finger traced a 27,000-mile line around the globe's fat middle.

"Alone?" called a voice from the crowd.

A.E. pointed out the man who was to accompany her. "I don't believe the pilot on such a flight can navigate too," she said.

"How long will your flight take?" asked another reporter.

"I have no estimate to give," she said. "Such a flight has never been attempted. I'll simply fly as and when I can, race nothing and nobody. . . . Every flight . . . is potentially important. It may yield valuable knowledge."

If anyone at the press conference had asked A.E. why she planned this dangerous trip, her likeliest answer would have been, "Just say I want to. Flying is fun—and one must take chances."

A.E. did not pack a toothbrush and take off.

Months of careful planning came before her press conference. She had to make up flight charts and draw her proposed course on them. She must know distances and terrain—where there were airfields and where emergency landings were out of the question. She must also know the prevailing winds in each region of the world, and what kind of weather to expect. Gasoline and oil had to be sent ahead to wait for her at each of the many places where she would stop to refuel. Spare parts had to be sent, too, for

Dakar or Calcutta or Singapore was not likely to have spare parts for an American-made plane.

Miss Earhart's plan was to circle the globe going west. But on the first lap of her trip, a tire blew while she was taking off from the Honolulu airport in Hawaii. Her plane swerved, the landing gear collapsed and both propellers were smashed.

Back to its California factory for repairs went the Electra, and A.E. went home to wait. This took three months, and in three months the seasons changed. A.E. had to study weather conditions all over again. Where would the dust storms and the monsoon winds be now? What about fogs and tropical rains? She decided it would be wiser this time to fly in a generally easterly direction.

A.E. piloted her repaired plane on a shake-down flight from California to Miami, Florida. Everything was in order.

It was dawn on June 1, 1937, when George Putnam stood on the Miami airfield, waving good-by to his wife and her navigator, Frederick J. Noonan, bound for California the longest way round. Fred Noonan had already crossed the Pacific eighteen times on commercial flights for Pan-American Airways. He was a veteran aerial navigator and transport pilot. Mrs. Beatrice Noonan, his bride of a month, was waiting in Oakland, California, for his return.

"Good luck!"

"See you in Oakland! We'll try to make it by the 4th of July!"

As Putnam watched the Electra disappear in the sky, he fingered a sealed envelope in his coat pocket. It was a letter he hoped never to open, for A.E.'s handwriting on the envelope said: "To be read only if I do not return."

Sky-borne, A.E. headed the Electra southeast toward Puerto Rico. She turned on her radio and listened to a Miami newscaster render a breathless account of her recent take-off. Turning to Noonan, she laughed happily. "When I was a little girl in Kansas," she said, "the adventures of travel fascinated me. My sister and I sat in an old abandoned carriage in the barn and we made all sorts of imaginary journeys full of fabulous perils. Now I'm still fascinated, but this isn't make-believe. We're really on our way!"

A.E. reached for her log book—it was really a secretary's dictation notebook—and made her first entry. She planned to write a book about her trip after it was over. So day after day, as her plane nibbled away at the miles that separated her from her destination, A.E. jotted down notes and mailed them back to her husband.

Here are some of the things she wrote:

[The Bahamas:] . . . Andros Island stretched out as a vivid green rug before our eyes. The fringe of that rug was formed by the varicolored tendrils of the sea reaching fingerlike into the islands. . . . we sighted a partly submerged wreck, mute testimony of a tragedy of long ago.

*The coast of Venezuela in the hazy distance was
my first glimpse of South America. As we drew near
I saw densely wooded mountains and between them
wide valleys of open plains and jungle. I had never
seen a jungle before. . . . jungles are in a pilot's
eyes about the least desirable of all possible landing
places.*

*Rain clouds hung thick about Caripito [Venezuela]
as we left on the morning of June third. We . . .
played hide-and-seek with showers until I decided I
had better forego the scenery . . . and climb up
through the clouds into fair weather. An altitude of
8,000 feet topped all but the highest woolly pin-
nacles. . . . As on this and many other days, the
pilot sees the rain slant against the land below. . . .
how many of the earthbound realize the relative
nearness of sunlight above the . . . gray dank world?*

*[Natal, Brazil:] At luncheon I could hardly realize
that I was in South America, for the food was so
like that at home—corn on the cob and apple pie
a la mode. . . . If this continues there will be no
keeping down our weight . . . Six added pounds
[aloft] offset one precious gallon of fuel.*

*As I write this, looking out the window I can see
two children playing in the sand.*

*On the evening of June 7, my Electra put her
wheels down in Africa, the third continent of our
journey. That leaves two more continents before us,
Asia and Australia.*

*[Dakar:] . . . Africa was to me a riot of human
color. . . . bright raiment . . . contrasted gaudily
with the neutral background of brown plains, bare
hills, parched vegetation and drab dwellings.*

[137]

Tomorrow, if all goes well, we start the long air route across Africa. . . . I am warned of tornadoes to the south and sandstorms on the north. So I must try to squeeze between.

So far our journey has been along established air lanes. . . . Now we turn . . . into regions where planes fly frequently but not on schedule.

Much of the terrain of that portion of Central Africa over which we flew is remarkably like the southwestern part of the United States. So much so that often it was almost necessary to pinch myself to realize how far from Arizona and New Mexico I actually had strayed. It is, of course, a hot country, with broad stretches of arid desert land, hemmed by regions rough and mountainous. And all beautiful.

From the heights we saw the Red Sea. It is not red, but blue. (Both the Blue Nile and the White Nile were green.) Beyond it we sighted a shimmering land of mirages that was Arabia.

One could scarcely imagine a more desolate region than that . . . shore [of the Arabian Sea] . . . Where rough mountains did not wet their feet in the sea, low sandhills rolled down to the water's edge. . . . Some regions looked as if mighty harrows had churned the badlands into a welter of razorback ridges, fantastic mountains and thirsty valleys barren of vegetation and devoid of life. . . .

In no part of southern Arabia is a forced landing desirable. . . . We carried . . . a pretty generous supply of water in canteens, concentrated foods, a small land compass, and very heavy walking shoes. Fortunately, we did not have to walk!

[Calcutta, India:] Driving from the airport to the home of our host, we saw many rickshas. The streets

were very wide and thronged with every kind of conveyance and with myriad white-clad figures. Small shops displayed wares next to tall office buildings. Bulls wandered at will on the sidewalks or in the streets, where Shirley Temple was showing in "Captain January."

[Singapore:] The vast city lies on an island, the broad expanses of its famous harbor filled, as I saw them from aloft that afternoon, with little water bugs, ships of all kinds from every port.

[Lae, New Guinea:] . . . my Electra now rests on the shores of the Pacific. . . . Somewhere beyond the horizon lies California. Twenty-two thousand miles have been covered so far. There are seven thousand more to go.

From Lae, A.E. and Noonan faced the longest single hop of their long trip—2,556 miles across the ocean where no plane had ever flown before. Their destination was Howland Island, a tiny dot of land two miles long and about a half-mile wide, rising only a few feet above the sea. The next nearest piece of land was Baker Island, another dot forty miles north. Aside from these sand bars there was nothing but water for hundreds of miles. Locating Howland Island in mid-Pacific was like aiming for a handkerchief lying in the middle of Texas. A.E. scribbled in her logbook: ". . . the whole width of the world has passed behind us—except this broad ocean. I shall be glad when we have the hazards of its navigation behind us."

To help A.E. locate Howland Island, the United

States Coast Guard cutter *Itasca* was standing by. Its duties were to keep in touch with A.E. by radio, giving her weather reports and homing signals to fly toward.

Her radio was not a strong one. She would have to fly on course for long hours before she came within hearing range of the *Itasca's* signals. There were no landmarks below to help Noonan check his course— only the stars above. Yet A.E. must guide the Electra with the utmost precision. If Noonan made a mistake of only one degree in his compass figuring, their plane would go one mile off course for every sixty miles it flew. At Lae the Electra's fifty-watt radio set was not functioning properly, and Fred Noonan had some trouble trying to set his chronometers.

A.E. cleared the airfield on Lae at ten o'clock in the morning of July 2, 1937. This was July 1 on Howland Island because the international date line lies at 180° of longitude in the mid-Pacific. A.E. thought she was flying into yesterday. She did not know she was really setting forth into eternity . . .

Even before A.E. might reasonably be within range of its radio, the *Itasca* began to send weather reports and homing signals to its charge up in the sky. Five crewmen crowded into the *Itasca's* tiny radio room, straining to hear A.E.'s voice acknowledging their signals. The air was full of static, making communication difficult. Head winds blew, cutting down the Electra's speed and increasing her fuel consumption.

About 2:45 A.M. they picked up her voice for the first time. All they could make out was, ". . . cloudy and overcast . . ."

Through the night the *Itasca* men struggled to keep in touch. Over the radio they told A.E. they could not catch her words. They asked her to switch to another wave length and tap out a code with her radio key. She did not do this, nor did she acknowledge the position bearings which the *Itasca* operator gave her over and over again. To the experienced radio men, this meant just one thing: the plane was having radio trouble.

Morning dawned—a clear, bright day. Commander W. K. Thompson, the *Itasca's* skipper, sent a detail of men ashore to scare off the thousands of sea birds resting on Howland Island so A.E. could come in safely. To serve as a guide, he ordered the engineer to send columns of heavy black smoke billowing out of the ship's funnels.

At 7:42 A.M. A.E.'s voice crackled over the radio: "We must be on you but cannot see you. Gas is running low. Been unable to reach you by radio. We are flying at altitude of 1,000 feet."

At 7:57: "We are circling but cannot see island. Cannot hear you."

The *Itasca* sent a long series of homing signals.

At 8:03: "Earhart calling *Itasca*. We received your signals but unable to get a minimum [for a bearing]."

The *Itasca* replied immediately, but received no acknowledgment. At 8:45 A.E.'s voice came through

for the last time. She was talking very fast: "We are
in line of position 157-337. Will repeat this message
. . . We are now running north and south . . ."

Her signal faded. Commander Thompson paced the
deck, surveying the open sky. Had the glare of the
rising sun blinded A.E. to his smoke signal? In his
judgment, she had overshot the tiny island and now
was flying out over the open sea with empty gas
tanks. At 9:00 A.M. he wired Washington: "Earhart
unreported   at   0900 . . . Believe   down . . . Am
searching probable area and will continue."

Admiral William D. Leahy, United States Chief of
Naval Operations, immediately instructed his services

to render all aid, and an enormous rescue effort began. As fast as they could fly or get up steam, airplanes and ships arrived: a battleship, a mine sweeper, an aircraft carrier, four destroyers, sixty-six airplanes. In widening circles, catapult planes combed every section of every tiny island for hundreds of miles around. Ships swept through more than 100,000 square miles of sea, empty except for the wreckage of an old tramp freighter. On July 7 two Japanese vessels joined the search. More than four thousand men were looking for Amelia Earhart and Fred Noonan, at a cost of a quarter of a million dollars a day. It was the biggest search in aviation history.

Back in Oakland, California, George Putnam kept day-and-night vigil and refused to abandon hope. "The plane's large wings and empty gas tanks should provide buoyancy," he said. "There was a two-man rubber lifeboat aboard the plane, as well as life belts, flares, and a large yellow signal kite which could be flown above the plane or the life raft. If they are down, they can stay afloat indefinitely."

On July 7 the mailman brought Beatrice Noonan a letter from her husband. It was postmarked "June 20." Noonan wrote, "Amelia is a grand person for such a trip. She is the only woman flier I would care to make such a trip with because in addition to being a fine companion she can take hardship as well as a man—and work like one."

Millions of people agreed that if courage meant

anything, Amelia Earhart would eventually turn up safe. Day after day, messages poured in from radio operators who claimed they were picking up A.E.'s distress signal, or her voice. Reports came from Honolulu, Los Angeles, San Francisco, Seattle, Cincinnati. Flares were sighted. Wreckage was seen. A friend with special spiritual powers claimed she could sense exactly where the plane was floating.

But no S.O.S. messages were heard on the powerful radios of the searching ships, and each patiently examined clue proved false. After a week, the chances of finding Earhart and Noonan were down to one in a million. On July 19th the official search was finally abandoned.

George Putnam opened his wife's letter and gave it to the world. It said:

"I want to do it because I want to do it. Women must try to do things as men have tried. When they fail, then failure must be but a challenge to others."

MARGARET MEAD

"The Whole World Is My Field"

1

On an early October morning in 1925, the steamship *Sonoma* dropped anchor in Pago-Pago. Only one passenger left ship at this port—a slim, brown-haired girl named Margaret Mead.

Margaret was just a fraction over five feet tall. With her bobbed hair and wide-spaced eyes, she looked entirely too young to be left alone on this tropical Samoan island in the South Seas, 13 degrees below the equator and 7,500 miles from her Pennsylvania home.

But actually Margaret was a twenty-three-year-old graduate student from Columbia University in New York City. She had earned a doctor's degree in anthropology and was now beginning her first field trip, an on-the-spot study of a people and their ways of living.

Margaret's exact assignment in Samoa was to study the lives of adolescent girls in this simple society. She was here to find out "whether they, like American girls, had years of tears and troubles before they were quite grown up."

Miss Mead had never stayed in a hotel before in her life. She checked into the only hotel in Pago-Pago and soon found out she was its only guest. The hotel was a ramshackle place, run by a shy native and his sad-eyed cook named Misfortune.

A little fearfully, Margaret unpacked her belongings: camera and typewriter, notebooks, a metal strongbox, a few clothes, and a blue silk baby pillow. She did not expect to be lonesome because she would be hard at work. First she would finish learning the beautiful, liquid-sounding Samoan language. Next she would get herself adopted into the household of a Samoan chief. Then, by actually living as a Samoan girl, she would learn with her heart as well as her mind how the girls grew into women.

How does Margaret Mead, or any person, find the road he wishes to follow in life? A child explores many paths while he grows. But the ways that are open to him depend on the place of his birth and the era in which he is born. The courses that he can see also depend on what kind of family he lives in, and what kind of dreams he dreams.

If Margaret Mead had been born in the early nineteenth century, like Susan B. Anthony, or if she had been born Negro, like Mary McLeod Bethune, the paths open to her would surely have been shorter, narrower ones. But Margaret was born on December 16, 1901. She was a twentieth-century girl, and she was raised in a household of highly educated, unusually gifted people.

Her mother, Emily Fogg, graduated from the University of Chicago. She had worked as a volunteer at Jane Addams' Hull-House before her marriage to Edward Sherwood Mead. The young couple settled in Philadelphia in order to be near the University of Pennsylvania, where Professor Mead taught economics.

Pretty Emily Mead did not abandon all her intellectual interests just because she was married and rearing a family. She continued to work and study, and raised her children in an atmosphere where girls, as well as boys, were free to follow their own interests. The Meads enjoyed a wide variety of friends and were unusually alive to the world around them. From her earliest childhood on, an interest in people seemed as natural to Margaret as breathing.

Professor Mead's widowed mother also lived in this lively household. Grandmother Mead had been a school teacher, and she, too, held unusual ideas. She taught the Mead children at home. Margaret and her younger brother Richard were close in age so they formed one class. Grandmother Mead's methods

would have made an ordinary teacher gasp. The
children studied botany, the science of plant life,
before they studied spelling. And they tackled algebra
ahead of arithmetic.

When Margaret was seven, her sister Elizabeth
was three and baby Priscilla was just beginning to
talk. Grandmother Mead gave Margaret her first
assignment in scientific observation and recording:
Margaret was to listen carefully and note all the new
words she heard in her little sisters' growing

vocabularies. Then she had to discover, if she could, which songs, stories or nursery rhymes had supplied the youngsters with their new words.

For instance, Grandmother Mead might say to Elizabeth, "You're looking pretty ragged today." If Elizabeth grinned and answered, "Because I'm the raggedy man," Margaret knew her younger sister had probably learned the word from a poem by James Whitcomb Riley:

> *O the Raggedy Man! He works fer Pa,*
> *An' he's the goodest man you ever saw!*

Since she was being taught at home, Margaret loved to visit friends in their "regular" school. Once, when she was ten, she went to school with a friend in Hinsdale, Illinois. The fourth graders were asked to write an essay on their favorite book. Margaret turned in a paper along with the other pupils.

Her favorite book just then was *Castle Blair* by Flora L. Shaw. It was an exciting story about the unusual adventures of five children who lived in a castle in Ireland. Margaret's essay fairly flowed off the end of her pencil.

A few days later the teacher said to the mother of Margaret's school friend, "Margaret wrote the most remarkable essay by a ten-year-old I've ever read."

This pleasant word quickly got back to Mrs. Mead and then, of course, to Margaret herself. She fondly decided to reread *Castle Blair*. But when she opened the book a paragraph leaped out like a slap. It was a quotation by a well-known English author, John Ruskin. To her amazement, she saw now that John Ruskin's prose was exactly what she had unconsciously put down as her own essay!

Margaret loved to read and write poetry. One poem by Robert Louis Stevenson cut a deeper path than others in her young mind. It went:

> *Dark brown is the river,*
>   *Golden is the sand;*
> *It flows along forever*
>   *With trees on either hand.*
>
> *Green leaves a-floating,*
>   *Castles on the foam,*
> *Boats of mine a-boating—*
>   *Where will all come home?*
>
>   *   *   *
>
> *Away down the river,*
>   *A hundred miles or more,*
> *Other little children*
>   *Shall bring my boats ashore.*

The Stevenson poem haunted Margaret, for it made her wonder, "What if nobody was there, further down the river, to see the leaf boats floating? Then they might never be brought ashore!" The same thing might happen to precious ideas, unless they were safely preserved in words or pictures.

At the same time she was troubled by another

notion. This one grew from the Bible parable about the exceedingly wicked man who wrapped his one talent up in a napkin and did nothing useful with it except bring it out again. Of course Margaret knew that in Biblical terms the word "talent" meant money. Years later she said, "I came from the kind of family that scarcely mentioned even taxes, except to say that they were not heavy enough to improve the schools as they ought to be improved, so it never occurred to me to dwell on the literal point of the parable—getting a return on money. I put people who did not use money responsibly and people who did not use their abilities to sing and write books together as people who put their talents in napkins."

Gradually Margaret began to realize "the obligation that was laid on each individual to use whatever gifts he had—to be very, very certain which they were and to use them wisely . . ."

Margaret began her formal schooling when she was eight. But the following year she came down with a severe case of whooping cough. While she recovered, her grandmother continued to teach her at home. Margaret painted and sewed and read widely and wrote plays. She said later, "I was a perfectly contented child . . ." But Grandmother Fogg, her maternal grandmother, provided a different description. She thought of Margaret at this time as "a tiresome child who was always writing long plays that nobody wanted to listen to."

Margaret started her college career at DePauw University in Greencastle, Indiana, where her father had studied. But at the end of her freshman year, in 1920, she transferred to Barnard College, part of Columbia University in New York. She was eager to study in a big university in a big city. There she could meet many different kinds of people and see customs which were new to her. She could enjoy forty plays a year if she wanted to, and write poetry and stay up half the night arguing with friends.

Margaret had a fine time in New York, majoring in English and doing all the big-city things she had hoped. But none of her college courses fully satisfied her endless curiosity about people. She wanted "to study peoples who live in the Arctic and in the tropics, on mountains and by the sea, in tiny tribes and in great kingdoms, those who knew nothing about reading and writing, and others who had kept records for thousands of years."

The summer Margaret was twenty, she spent her college vacation at home. Her family was then living in Buckingham Township, Pennsylvania. With typical energy, Margaret threw herself into writing and directing an elaborate pageant, *The Spirit of Buckingham Valley*. There were parts in it for every child in the township. Members of the women's club stitched bright cheesecloth costumes, and one of Margaret's college friends came down to organize the dances.

The performance, scheduled for the end of summer, took place in a beautiful open meadow. At the last moment an enthusiastic parent decided to mow the field. His sharp scythe cut down the tall grass and wild flowers which might have been in the children's way. But it also tumbled quantities of freshly cut poison ivy into the ditch where the children were to wait their turn to go on stage.

That year the Buckingham Township schools opened a week late. Most of their pupils were at home with poison ivy.

In her senior year at Barnard, Margaret took a course from Dr. Franz Boas in the Department of

Anthropology. The subject excited her from the first day, and soon she knew she had found her path.

The science of anthropology is an immense field because it studies man's place in nature. It is interested in the beginnings and the growth and the differences and similarities of all the people of the world, from the dawn of history to this very moment.

There are many subdivisions a student of anthropology can choose to follow. He can excavate the remains of past civilizations. He can study the varying physical characteristics of the races of mankind. Some anthropologists trace the spread of customs or religions over the face of the earth; others work to define the hundreds of languages to learn how these tongues differ and how they are related.

Among these areas of work, Margaret Mead was especially interested in cultural anthropology. A people's culture includes not only music and art, but all their ways of living together. An anthropologist is trained to observe the details that make up a pattern of life. He notes how a marriage is arranged, a committee organized, a funeral conducted. He sees the way people cook their food, and whether children or old people receive the larger portions. While he learns whether a people serves food mushy or chewy, whether they feast together or turn their backs while they eat, he is also looking for the patterns of belief which lie under the way people behave.

Just about the time Margaret was discovering anthropology, she happened to read a book called

The Mystery of Easter Island. Its author, Mrs. Scoresby Routledge, was curious about some puzzling statues that stood on Easter Island. She organized an expedition to sail to the tiny island, hoping to talk with a native who could tell her about the strange legends written on the backs of the statues. But when Mrs. Routledge, after many difficulties, finally arrived on Easter Island, the last man who could have told her anything about the statues was mortally ill. He died two weeks later, and the answers to the statues died with him.

This book gave Margaret a sense of urgency about plunging into her work. Dr. Franz Boas and his assistant, Dr. Ruth Benedict, also knew that time was running out for the small, simple cultures that existed on the edges of the modern world. People like Amelia Earhart were rapidly developing travel by air, and soon the world would have no more edges. Planes would poke the long finger of civilization into every remaining corner, and destroy ancient ways of life as surely as a human finger disturbs the pattern of a cobweb.

Margaret wanted to preserve some written records of these ways of life before the primitive societies disappeared forever. There were nights when she could hardly sleep for worrying because she knew there were no "other little children to bring my boats ashore." She persuaded Professor Boas that her first field trip would be to Samoa.

But exactly how does an anthropologist go about

studying people in their culture? Years later, in a
book written for children, *People and Places*, Dr.
Mead explained: "If someone wants to see if it is
true that a certain kind of fertilizer makes more
beans grow, he can put fertilizer on one half of his
experimental garden and not on the other half. Then
even if more beans grow in the fertilized part of the
garden, no one need feel sorry for the unfertilized
part. . . . No one needs to think about the beans'
feelings. Nor need anyone fear that such an experiment
will turn the gardener into a cruel man."

Studying human beings is not so easy. "We could
not point telescopes at them to watch them, nor
could we put them all together in a giant glass jar
to watch them as fruit flies are watched. We had
no instruments to look inside them to see what
happened in their brains when they tried to solve
a problem or in their blood stream when they were
angry or frightened. . . . Nor could we get left-handed
men to marry left-handed girls . . . to find out
whether their children would be left-handed . . ."

Every anthropologist, however, has one tool—himself. ". . . a man watching another man can understand something about how he feels, and if he learns
the other man's language he can ask him questions
and listen to his answers. So the study of human
beings in many parts of the world began with men
and women . . . who asked questions."

To cover the expenses of her field trip to Samoa,

Margaret secured a grant of money from a scientific organization. But the National Research Council did not provide money for traveling expenses. There would be a train ride across the continent from New York to San Francisco, and then a two-week trip by steamer across more than four thousand miles of ocean.

Professor Mead, who had always encouraged his daughter, did so again. He gave her a thousand dollars to buy tickets for the voyage. "A project which adds to the sum of exact knowledge in the world is worth doing," he said.

Advice poured in from all sides. "Wait a few years before you take on such a big job." "Let me get you an introduction to the chief medical officer at the United States Naval Station in Pago-Pago, so he can keep an eye on you." "Don't eat raw pork or rotten fish."

Margaret accepted an introduction to the chief medical officer and assured her friends she had absolutely no desire to eat rotten fish. It was only after the S.S. *Matsonia* was churning across the Pacific Ocean toward Honolulu that she remembered a Barnard professor's excellent advice. Dr. Henry Crampton was a zoologist who had traveled widely in the South Seas and knew what he was talking about. "Take a little pillow with you," he had said, "and you'll be able to sleep wherever you are."

From the time the *Matsonia* landed in Honolulu until the *Sonoma* sailed for Samoa, Margaret was the

guest of one of her mother's college friends. When
Margaret wanted to buy herself a pillow the hostess
said, "Let me get one for you." And she did—a lovely
blue silk thing, meant for a baby's carriage.

"You insisted it had to be small!" said the friend.

2

Little wonder that Margaret unpacked her pillow and other few belongings in a cloud of excitement touched with uneasiness. Here she was in a run-down hotel in Samoa, thousands of miles from home and with only $4.50 in her purse. She devoutly hoped another fellowship check would arrive by the next mail boat.

And with all her heart she prayed for success in the big project that lay ahead. For she was attempting a different kind of field work on a different kind of problem from what anyone, man or woman, had ever done before. She planned "to become a Samoan girl as nearly as possible, to learn to eat their food, sleep on their mats, share their jests and above all share their manners. Just as the only way to explore a cave is to enter it, so the only way in which I could be sure of knowing how a Samoan girl acted, was to try to act that way myself."

The very next day Margaret plunged into her work. A soft-voiced native nurse named Butterfly gave her lessons in Samoan.

"Talofa," said Butterfly, "means 'love to thee.'" Or she might ask Margaret to say, "Sleep thou, and life to thee."

Then Margaret would reply, "Tofa soi fua."

But Margaret made many mistakes. It was so difficult to learn a Polynesian language that was not related to any modern civilized tongue! Just to accent the second syllable of a word instead of the third changed its whole meaning. Once Margaret thought she was saying, "Samoan is very difficult," but later Butterfly giggled and told her she had really said, "The Samoan language is very vaccination." No wonder the people she had been talking to had looked so blank!

In Samoan the word for "light" and the word for "understanding" are the same: "Malamalama." For six hard weeks Margaret worked toward "malamalama." But she often said under her breath, "I can't do it! I can't do it!" Then one day she noticed she was saying "I can't do it!" in Samoan, not English, and she knew she could do it.

Now Margaret was ready to leave Pago-Pago for the village of the Turtle and the Shark. Its chief, Ufuti, had agreed to receive her into his house as his guest. One of Chief Ufuti's many relatives, a half-caste woman with tiny gold rings in her ears, escorted Margaret to the village.

The village of the Turtle and the Shark was located on the west coast of the island of Tau. It was made up of a cluster of dwellings nicely placed among groves of palm, breadfruit, and mango trees. The houses had round roofs of sugar-cane thatch, rather like beehives, resting on pillars of wood. The houses had no walls. Down near the edge of the sea Margaret noticed several roofs that were larger than the others. Her guide explained that these were guest houses of the chiefs. They were called "houses to meet the stranger."

But kind-faced Chief Ufuti did not meet Margaret as a stranger. He greeted her at the door of his own home. Margaret saw Sava, the plump and dimpled lady who was Chief Ufuti's wife. There were also a daughter, Fa'amotu, two sons, a baby boy, a small girl named Tulip, and several guests from another island.

Here, in front of all these waiting people, Margaret had to go through the ceremony of politeness for which Butterfly had so carefully coached her during the past difficult weeks.

It began with Chief Ufuti saying, "May you most honorably enter."

In a courteous singing tone Margaret replied, "I have humbly come saving the presence of your lordship and her who sits in the back of the house."

"Alas for the coming hither of your ladyship," said Chief Ufuti. "There is nothing good in the house."

"Oh, let the matter rest," replied Margaret, "it is of no consequence whatever."

Margaret was so nervous she sang her responses incorrectly. Heaven only knew what she might really be saying! But Chief Ufuti graciously noticed nothing. A fresh coconut was served to her, and Margaret was accepted as a daughter of the household. From now on her name was not Margaret, but Makelita.

When it was time for sleep, the women took thin

woven mats from the rafters. Makelita was to share a bed with her new "sister," Fa'amotu. The girls piled mat upon mat, until their bed was raised several inches above the gray pebbles of the floor. Makelita politely did not use her little silk pillow, since Fa'amotu brought out snowy linen and two white pillows for the bed. Makelita's pillow was beautifully embroidered with red roses but it was hard as a dry sponge.

Next the girls unrolled mosquito netting which was slung from stout cord in the rafters. They used heavy stones to weight the netting on the ground. Chief Ufuti hung a wide curtain of bark cloth between the girls' corner and the rest of the house. Later Makelita realized he did this as a special courtesy because of her "unusual" American ideas about privacy. Samoans had no need for walls. When a person dressed or combed his hair, others simply looked away.

So Makelita retired. There was only the mosquito netting between her room and the rest of the village, but at least it keep out the village's wandering dogs, pigs, and chickens. Makelita tossed about on her hard bed until she found a comfortable position on her back. Then, listening to rhythmic sea noises, she fell asleep.

From that first night, Makelita was accepted as a Samoan girl. In the morning she helped to put the bed mats back up onto the rafters of the house.

Using a stiff, short-handled broom she swept the floor of water-worn coral pebbles. She soon learned to sit cross-legged on a mat, and to eat with her fingers from a mat. She became skilled in weaving these coarse mats, which were in constant use as tables, beds, and chairs.

Ufuti assigned Lolo, the talking chief, to teach Makelita the manners a Samoan girl should know. She learned that speaking on one's feet within the house was unforgivably rude. She learned to sit cross-legged for hours without squirming or complaining. Lolo was a jolly man who laughed at Makelita's mistakes. But if she did not correct them at once, or if she failed too often, he became very stern.

In Samoa all the babies were taken care of by girls between the ages of six and ten. The older girls went into the plantations with their mothers to cultivate sugar cane and taro. Or they fished for crabs along the reefs at low tide. When a girl was about twelve she would begin the weaving of one especially large, fine mat which would be her trousseau when she married. It took many years to complete such a mat, but no girl was in a hurry to finish it. In fact, hurrying was bad manners. The Samoans called it, "Talking above your age."

Life in the village of the Turtle and the Shark was very pleasant. But Makelita had to meet other people in other villages. It was time to move on.

The leaders of the village of the Turtle and the

Shark called a solemn meeting. The most important men sat in privileged positions near the house posts, where they could lean their backs. Minor officials had to sit unsupported on the open floor.

Years later Dr. Mead described the meeting: ". . . I had to sit cross-legged, with a perfectly straight back, and arms severely folded. No matter how many flies flew trustfully under my chin . . . I must not move a finger to brush them away . . .

"The worst question of all came at the end. A very old chief leaned forward slightly and asked, 'Why is it that you have elected to spend only two weeks here in this village and plan, so it is said, to go to the faraway islands of Manu'a and spend six months?' The atmosphere was very tense. I hastily arranged my nouns, verbs, and alibis in my head, and answered a little breathlessly: 'If it please your lordship, when I planned to go to Manu'a I had not yet seen the village of the Turtle and the Shark.'

"Everyone relaxed and one man muttered to another, 'The proper courtesy answer.' And I was saved."

For many months Makelita continued her careful study of the fifty girls who lived on three coastal villages of the island of Tau in Manu'a Archipelago. With the other girls, Makelita cultivated sugar cane and brought coral rubble from the seashore to sprinkle over the floor. She wove garlands of flowers and danced to the chanting of voices and the soft clapping of hands at twilight. She walked barefoot over the sandy beaches and went fishing at night by torchlight. She ate taro and green banana baked in hot ashes. She ate eel and land crabs and raw tuitui fish that tasted like custard. To her amazement, rotten fish was as delicious as expensive cheese. In fact, she couldn't believe it really was rotten. She found herself taking just one more bite "to make sure."

During this time, Makelita filled page after page of her notebook with details about the girls and their families. She came to know how they spent their days and nights, and who their best friends were; what they thought about themselves, and about growing up and getting married. She drew little sketches in her notebook to show how a pattern was traced onto bark cloth, or how to use an eel trap.

One day Makelita went on a visit to the island of Ofu, twelve miles away. Her friends, Braided Roses and Born-in-three-houses, came along. The three girls wrapped wet cloths around their heads to protect themselves from the scorching sun. But the boys who rowed the slender outrigger canoe protected their heads with a thick layer of slaked lime. While the lime kept them from sunstroke it would also be bleaching their hair to a fashionable pale yellow.

By the time their canoe touched shore on the island of Ofu the sun had set, and a fine, misty rain was falling. But high chief Misa had planned a reception in their honor to be held that very evening.

Makelita dressed herself in an expertly woven mat skirt. She wore a tight bodice and a broad sash of white-bark cloth. She rubbed her skin with scented coconut oil and balanced a bright hibiscus flower behind her ear. Then she joined in the singing and the dancing.

Suddenly Misa's talking chief spoke to Makelita. "The honorable lady of Misa [his wife] has most honorable slipped away [died]," he said. "Misa is rich. He will marry your highness and accompany you on your further travels around the world."

At once Makelita felt she was Margaret Mead, a stranger. The music and dancing had stopped. She sat in a circle of dark, expectant faces and wondered what she could reply. Would she end up repaying the kindness of these people by insulting their chief? Of course the offer was not meant seriously. Yet here were the assembled people, and they were waiting formally for her to answer.

There was a long silence. Then Makelita answered carefully, "When I left my home in America I said that I was going all around the world by myself. All the people laughed and said that a mere girl could not go around the world by herself.

"Were I to accept his lordship Misa's most honorable invitation and were he to accompany me, all the people would laugh and say that they had been right. And I would be ashamed because I who was young had boasted of something which I could not perform."

The tension relaxed and the crisis was over. Again Makelita had given the courteous answer.

At last Margaret Mead said good-by to her "brothers and sisters," "relatives" and friends in Samoa. She returned to New York and joined the staff of the American Museum of Natural History. Here, sitting in a small office up under the eaves, she set about turning her mass of notes into a book.

The book described how peacefully Samoan girls grew up. They did not suffer the stresses and strains most American girls know, because their culture did

not pull them this way and that with conflicting goals. *Coming of Age in Samoa* was so interestingly written, and its ideas were so fresh to many American minds, that it quickly became a best seller.

But long before she knew how popular her book would be, young Dr. Mead and her blue baby pillow had left the country on another field trip. This time they visited the sweltering Admiralty Islands, north of New Guinea. Although she was ill with malaria about a third of the time, Dr. Mead studied the Manus children, faithfully observed Manus taboos, and learned to use shells and dogs' teeth for money.

Again she was able to write a book about a vanishing society. *Growing Up in New Guinea* described the brown-skinned Manus people who lived in houses built on stilts over the sea and raised their children to become worried, money-minded businessmen like themselves.

As the years went by the tools of anthropology grew to include fast film, movie cameras, and tape recorders. But the basic equipment continued to be an open mind and a questing spirit.

Margaret Mead studied three more New Guinea tribes. She found the Arapesh people were peaceable, humorous, and loving toward their children. On the other hand, the angry Mundugumor adults treated children roughly and raised them to become headhunters and cannibals like themselves. Among the Tchambuli the men arranged their hair in delicate curls, walked with mincing steps, and loved to carve beautiful wooden objects. The women were the ones who chose their mates and held the purse strings.

In March, 1936, Dr. Mead was married to an English anthropologist, Gregory Bateson. After their wedding the couple traveled to Bali. Dr. Mead made her usual careful study of the way Balinese children grew up, while Dr. Bateson took 28,000 photographs and thousands of feet of motion pictures.

The couple's only child, Mary Catherine Bateson, was born in New York in 1939. Like her mother before her, Margaret Mead now had to balance the claims of family life against those of her work.

As her own mother had done when she was an infant, Dr. Mead kept a "baby book." Like her mother's record, it contained much more than the usual information about Catherine's first tooth and first step. It described her behavior as she developed—such things as what she did when she first noticed a dog, or how she acted when she was angry, or the way she accepted a strange food. When Catherine was old enough to write, Dr. Mead taught her daughter—as she herself had been taught—to observe details carefully and note them down accurately.

Dr. Mead shared a household with friends, who provided a home for Catherine when her mother was away. During World War II, for instance, Dr. Mead served as an adviser to the United States government. During those years of food shortages she studied the ways in which people develop tastes for certain foods. Through such a study, she hoped to be able to suggest ways in which these tastes might be changed.

In 1953, when Catherine was fourteen, Dr. Mead again undertook a major field trip. She made a return visit to the Manus people whom she had studied twenty-five years earlier.

In the course of thirty-seven years, Dr. Mead took nine major field trips and learned seven South Sea languages. She published dozens of books and articles. She became a popular lecturer all over the United States, Europe, and Australia, sometimes delivering eighty talks a year. She also continued her work with the American Museum of Natural History and taught anthropology at Columbia University.

Many of Dr. Mead's findings upset long-held ideas, for she taught that it is not "human nature" but custom which causes us to organize our family life and raise our children as we do. The vividly different people of the world, in the endless variety of their customs, are really all doing the same *kinds* of things: "They marry and bring up their children. They know how to find food and how to keep order and how to give their children some idea of what man is."

She realized that all people, no matter where or when they lived, no matter how simple their society, were first of all human beings like herself. "Though they knew nothing about writing or higher mathematics or the natural sciences or the great religions,

[174]

the differences between what they are and what I am," she said, "have come about because of what I was able to learn in a highly civilized society and what they were able to learn in a little faraway society."

These discoveries of anthropology serve as hopeful signposts to the future. To know that the peoples of the world are infinitely varied but that people everywhere are the same is a giant step toward tolerance and peace on earth.

AFTERWORD

Only eighty-one years lie between the birth of Susan B. Anthony and the birth of Margaret Mead. The time interval is so short that the first woman in this book could have been grandmother to the last. But their lifetimes spanned such enormous changes that, seen another way, Miss Anthony and Dr. Mead scarcely shared the same world.

For not only are present-day women allowed to vote and ride bicycles; they have almost unbelievable freedom to enjoy nearly every kind of occupation and activity open to human beings. They are even free to choose the stay-at-home role that was once forced upon them!

Imagine the sparkle in Susan B. Anthony's eyes if she could return today. Truly she would discover that "the old doors have swung wide on their hinges."

BIBLIOGRAPHY

SUSAN B. ANTHONY

Boynick, David K. *Pioneers in Petticoats*. New York: Thomas Y. Crowell Company, 1959.

Daugherty, Sonia V. *Ten Brave Women*. Philadelphia: J. B. Lippincott Company, 1953.

Harper, Ida Husted. *The Life and Work of Susan B. Anthony, A Story of the Evolution of the Status of Women*. 3 volumes. Indianapolis: The Bowen-Merrill Company, Volumes I and II, 1898; Volume III, 1908.

Lutz, Alma. *Susan B. Anthony: Rebel, Crusader, Humanitarian*. Boston: Beacon Press, 1959.

JANE ADDAMS

Addams, Jane. *Twenty Years at Hull-House*. New York: The MacMillan Company, 1924. Paperback edition: New American Library.

Judson, Clara Ingram. *City Neighbor; The Story of Jane Addams*. New York: Charles Scribner's Sons, 1951.

Linn, James Weber. *Jane Addams, A Biography*. New York: Appleton-Century Company, Inc., 1935.

Sandburg, Carl. *Abraham Lincoln*. Volume I: *The Prairie Years*. New York: Harcourt, Brace and World, Inc., 1926. Paperback edition: Dell Publishing Company.

Weinberg, Arthur M., and Lila (Editors). *The Muckrakers: The Era in Journalism That Moved America to Reform*. New York: Simon and Schuster, Inc., 1961.

Wise, Winifred E. *Jane Addams of Hull-House*. New York: Harcourt, Brace and World, Inc., 1935.

New York *Times,* May 22, 1935.

BIBLIOGRAPHY

MARY MC LEOD BETHUNE

Peare, Catherine Owens. *Mary McLeod Bethune.* New York: Vanguard Press, 1951.

Richardson, Ben Albert. *Great American Negroes.* New York: Thomas Y. Crowell Company, 1956.

Sterne, Emma Gelders. *Mary McLeod Bethune.* New York: Alfred A. Knopf, Inc., 1957.

Current Biography Yearbook, 1942. New York: The H. W. Wilson Company.

Newsweek, May 30, 1955, p. 57.

Time, March 7, 1949, p. 44; May 30, 1955, p. 44.

New York *Times,* May 19, 1955; May 20, 1955; May 24, 1955.

AMELIA EARHART

Briand, Paul L., Jr. *Daughter of the Sky: The Story of Amelia Earhart.* New York: Duell, Sloan and Pearce, 1960.

Earhart, Amelia (Arranged by George Palmer Putnam). *Last Flight.* New York: Harcourt, Brace and World, Inc., 1937.

Garst, Doris Shannon. *Amelia Earhart, Heroine of the Skies.* New York: Julian Messner, Inc., 1947.

Putnam, George Palmer. *Soaring Wings; A Biography of Amelia Earhart.* New York: Harcourt, Brace and World, Inc., 1939.

New York *Herald Tribune,* July 2-8, 1937.

New York *Times,* July 3-12, 1937.

Elliott, Lawrence. "The Mystery of Amelia Earhart's Last Flight," *Reader's Digest,* July 1957, pp. 110-16.

Time, July 12, 1937, pp. 50-51; July 19, 1937, pp. 45-46; July 26, 1936, p. 36.

MARGARET MEAD

Clymer, Eleanor, and Erlich, Lillian. *Modern American Career Women.* New York: Dodd, Mead and Company, 1959.

Mead, Margaret. *From the South Seas.* New York: William Morrow and Company, Inc., 1939. Contains three of Miss Mead's books: *Coming of Age in Samoa; Growing Up in New Guinea; Sex and Temperament in Three Primitive Societies.* Paperback editions of each title are published by Apollo Editions, Inc., and New American Library.

――――. "Life as a Samoan Girl" in *All True! The Record of Actual Adventures That Have Happened to Ten Women of Today.* New York: Brewer, Warren and Putnam, 1931.

――――. "One Aspect of Male and Female" in *Women, Society and Sex,* edited by Johnson E. Fairchild. New York: Sheridan House, 1952. Paperback edition: Premier Books.

――――. *People and Places.* Cleveland: The World Publishing Company, 1959. Paperback edition: Bantam Books, Inc.

Yost, Edna. *American Women of Science.* Philadelphia and New York: Frederick A. Stokes, 1943.

Current Biography Yearbook, 1951. New York: The H. W. Wilson Company.

Mead, Margaret. "My First Job," *Ladies Home Journal,* April 1957, p. 199.

――――. "Return of the Cave Woman," *Saturday Evening Post,* March 3, 1962, p. 6.

――――. "The Secret of Completeness," *Good Housekeeping,* May 1960, p. 72.

――――. "Cultural Aspects of Women's Vocational Problems in Post World War II," *Journal of Consulting Psychology,* Volume X (1946), No. 1.

――――. "Cultural Bases for Understanding Literature." Publications of the Modern Language Association of America, LXVIII (April 1953), No. 2.

BIBLIOGRAPHY

————. "The Immortality of Man," *Pastoral Psychology,* June 1957.

————. "Moments of Personal Discovery." Religion and Civilization Series. Edited by R. M. MacIver and published by The Institute for Religious and Social Studies; distributed by Harper and Bros.

Sargeant, Winthrop. "Profile," *The New Yorker,* December 30, 1961, pp. 31–4.

INDEX

INDEX

ABOUT THE AUTHOR

DOROTHY NATHAN is a liberal arts graduate of the University of California, and she also holds a master's degree in education. She has worked in a social agency and as a teacher, but the greater part of her adult life has gone into raising three children and participating in voluntary activities connected with such organizations as the Child Study Association of America, the League of Women Voters, and the P.T.A.

The Nathans live in the country outside New York City. Their house has two studies because both Dorothy and Paul Nathan are writers. So are their sons Andrew and Carl, now studying at Harvard, and their daughter Janet, who attends high school. The only non-writing talent in the family belongs to Nathan, the cat.

Mrs. Nathan has always been interested in individual lives and curious about the qualities and circumstances that shape their course. As far back as she can remember she has wanted to be a writer. This is her first book.

ABOUT THE ILLUSTRATOR

CAROLYN CATHER studied art history while attending Duke University, at Durham, North Carolina, and later learned to draw while working for the newspaper *Stars and Stripes* in Japan after World War II. As a child she traveled all over the world. Her father was an army officer, and the family lived in many different places, including Japan and the Philippines.

After leaving her job in Japan she lived for a while in Holland, where her daughter was able to go ice skating on the canals because of an unusually cold winter. They presently live in New York City, where Carolyn Cather has been busily engaged providing illustrations for such travel books as *Cook's Tour of San Francisco* and *Cook's Tour of Rome*.

U.S. LANDMARK BOOKS